WHO SWITCHED OFF

MY
BRAIN?

controlling toxic thoughts and emotions

You can learn to control your thought life
dr. caroline leaf

SWITCH ON YOUR BRAIN (Ltd.)

For further information, call, write or email:
Switch On Your Brain at +1-817-404-9469 or info@drleaf.com

Printed in the USA

2140 E Southlake Blvd.
Suite L#809
Southlake, TX 76092

ISBN: 978-0-9833462-8-9

Design: Switch On Your Brain
Illustrations: Riccardo Capecchi

Scripture references from *New King James Version* of the Bible. Copyright © 1985 by Thomas Nelson Publishers.

Disclaimer: The information and solutions offered in this book are intended to serve as guidelines for managing toxic thoughts, emotions and bodies. Please discuss specific symptoms and medical conditions with your doctor.

SWITCH ON YOUR BRAIN INTERNATIONAL LLC

DEDICATION

To Jesus Christ:
My Lord and Savior, my source of
inspiration and strength

To my husband, Mac:
My ever-present loving support, you are an
outstanding example of controlling
toxic thoughts and emotions

To my children:
Jessica, Dominique, Jeffrey-John and Alexandria,
you are my absolute joy and a
complete guide to detoxing

ACKNOWLEDGEMENTS

I acknowledge all the special people who helped me with this book:

My wonderful husband, Mac, who put up with many hours of me burning the candle through the night, and who was always there to encourage and guide me. Your invaluable insight and constant, unwavering love carries me more than you realize. Thank you as well for all the time poured into proofreading. I love you forever.

My wonderful children, Jessica, Dominique, Jeffrey-John and Alexy, who patiently waited for me to write, giving up hours of "with-mom time" so I could finish this book. Your kisses and hugs of encouragement warmed my heart and carried me through the long hours. I love you forever.

My special editor, manuscript consultant and friend, Marika. You walked this journey with me with such excitement and passion. Thank you for doing an excellent job in record time.

To Wendy, nothing ever seemed too much for you. Thank you for your willingness and positive attitude throughout. You've been amazing and so professional.

To Ric, once again you have managed to capture my ideas in your creative mind. Thanks for the gorgeous illustrations.

And to my special friends, Ann and Peter, thank you for your support and belief in me.

CONTENTS

INTRODUCTION

Since 1981, I have researched the human brain with particular emphasis on unlocking its vast untapped potential. After teaching courses to more than 80,000 students in South Africa, I have no doubt that you can improve your life by understanding the scientific fact that fear is harmful but faith can set you free. Science is proving what the Bible has taught us all along.

My passion is to help you reach your God-given potential. This book will teach you how to achieve your potential by cleansing your thought life of toxic emotions.

In fact:
You can think yourself clever.
You can think yourself calm.
You can think yourself healthy.
You can think yourself out of worry and anxiety.
You can think yourself out of bitterness and resentment.
You can think yourself into forgiving.
You can think yourself in control of your emotions.
You can think yourself out of stress.

The verdict of science is in: the mind-body connection is real. No longer can we relegate those so-called psychosomatic disorders to the dark corners of the mind.

Behavior starts with a thought. Thoughts stimulate emotions which then result in attitude and finally produce behavior. This symphony of electrochemical reactions in the body affects the way we think and feel physically. Therefore, toxic thoughts produce toxic emotions, which produce toxic attitudes, resulting in toxic behavior.

The good news? These toxic thoughts, emotions and attitudes are controllable! And that means your physical and emotional well-being are controllable, too.

You can learn how to control your thought life and consequently your emotions, attitudes and behavior, ultimately leading to feeling and living better.

This book is a detox manual that describes the anatomy of a thought and the influence it has over emotions and attitudes. Understanding how it all works helps you learn how to control and change your thought life so that the resulting behaviors can change as well.

So go ahead and detox!

1CHAPTER ONE
THE ANATOMY OF A THOUGHT

What's in a thought? More than you probably know. Every thought has a corresponding electrochemical reaction in your brain. When you think, chemicals course through your body in magnificently complex electrochemical feedback loops. These chemicals produce electromagnetic waves which, if you could hear them, would sound like the most exquisite orchestral symphony.

At any one moment, your brain is creatively performing about 400 billion actions, of which you are only conscious of around 2,000. Each of these harmoniously regulated actions has both a chemical and an electrical component that are responsible for triggering emotions.

When you feel happy, your brain has released specific types of chemicals or neurotransmitters called endorphins or "feel-good chemicals." The brain releases endorphins in response to pleasurable feelings like those of a woman eating a decadent piece of Belgian chocolate. Exercise also prompts the release of endorphins which is why physical activity is often touted as being anti-depressive.

> **At any one moment, your brain is creatively performing about 400 billion actions, of which you are only conscious of around 2,000.**

When you feel sad, afraid, angry or hopeful, your brain releases different types of chemicals. In fact, your brain can be compared to a prolific factory producing a variety of chemicals depending on what type of emotion you are experiencing.

Depending on whether or not these emotions are toxic to your body, the chemicals will either help you or harm you. If they are harmful, they create conditions for a host of health problems that will manifest in both the body and the mind. Emotions that regularly release a torrent of destructive chemicals that will be the most damaging over time are: unforgiveness, anger, rage, resentment, depression, worry, anxiety, frustration, fear, excessive grief and guilt.

Research shows that around 87% of illnesses can be attributed to our thought life, and approximately 13% to diet, genetics and environment. Studies conclusively link more chronic diseases (also known as lifestyle diseases) to an epidemic of toxic emotions in our culture. These toxic emotions can cause migraines, hypertension, strokes, cancer, skin problems, diabetes, infections and allergies, just to name a few. Despite all the marvels of modern high-tech medicine and decades of innovative research, these illnesses are increasing worldwide.

> **Research shows that around 87% of illnesses can be attributed to our thought life, and approximately 13% to diet, genetics and environment. Studies conclusively link more chronic diseases (also known as lifestyle diseases) to an epidemic of toxic emotions in our culture.**

Even more frightening is that medical science has directly linked emotions, such as depression, to an increased risk of cancer and heart disease. Studies also point to a direct correlation between anxiety/fear and heart palpitations, irritable bowel syndrome, tension headaches and heart problems.

Quite simply, there is no longer any doubt that what and how you think affect your emotional and physical state. The mind and body are integrally connected.

The theory behind the existence of a dynamic information network linking mind and body is both provocative and revolutionary. Surprising to most people is that thought life, attitudes, habits and emotions are largely responsible for mental and physical health. Thoughts deep within the mind – along with their corresponding minute, biochemical reactions – have a massive impact on emotional and physical wellness.

> **The mind and body are integrally connected.**

If you doubt this fact, just look around. How many people appear to be in excellent health, but after going though a stressful event (death of a loved one, a bitter divorce, a job loss), were "suddenly" diagnosed with heart problems, breathing problems, hypertension or a range of other ailments?

What about you? Have you ever become ill in the wake of a difficult or traumatic time in your life? You may not have made the connection, just chalking it up to coincidence. It was more likely to be the result of toxic thoughts taking their toll on your health.

It is normal to have stress in your life; however, your body is not naturally designed to cope with an avalanche of it. Thus, your body is averse to the constant stream of stress that flows from toxic thoughts and feelings.

Interestingly, stress does not only come from unpleasant events. Ask any mother of the bride, or even the bride and bridegroom, how their health seemed to take a turn for the worse after the intensity of such a happy occasion.

Dr. Candace Pert is a pioneering neuroscientist whose work demonstrates without doubt that there is a biomolecular basis for our emotions. She bases her work on the theory that the body and mind function as a single psychosomatic network, which comprises information molecules that control our physical and mental health.

Pert's compelling conclusion is that emotions and their biological components establish the crucial link between the mind and the body. She has called these biochemicals "molecules of emotion" (also the title of her book), and rightly so. These information molecules carry a literal photocopy of the thought formulated in the depths of the memory networks of your brain. Dr. Marion Diamond, another groundbreaking brain researcher, calls these memory networks the "magic trees of the mind."

> Pert's compelling conclusion is that emotions and their biological components establish the crucial link between the mind and the body.

In effect, these networks create "copies" of your "thought life" along with the emotions that the chemicals coursing through your bloodstream literally carry around your whole body like an information highway. Information molecules are then able to cause changes at the cellular level, actually restructuring the cell's makeup on the outside and the DNA on the inside. This is how diseases are able to take hold in the body.

For example, if you have been repeatedly verbally abused by someone at work, or if you were sexually abused as a child, all the thoughts associated with those experiences will release negative chemicals. These chemicals travel through your body and can change the shape of the receptors on cells lining your heart, thereby increasing your susceptibility to cardiovascular illness.

The converse is also true: if you have been repeatedly recognized and praised at work, at school and at home, positive chemicals are released and distributed through the body which make positive changes to cells and DNA. They actually enhance your ability to build memory, develop intelligence and boost your immune system to help you stay healthy longer.

> Negative reinforcement releases negative chemicals. Positive reinforcement releases positive chemicals.

As you can see, the right thoughts help nurture and create a positive stronghold in the magic memory trees of the mind. Consequently, these positive thoughts strengthen positive feedback loops and release biochemicals such as endorphins, enkephalins and serotonin from the brain's natural pharmacy. Bathed in these environments, intellect flourishes, and with it mental and physical health.

> Your thoughts can de-stress you, making you
> more clever, calm and in control of your
> emotions, or they can do just the opposite!
> The choice is yours.

Before you can think yourself well, you need to have some insight into the actual thought pathways by which you can think yourself well or ill. When you first start to develop a thought by building memory, it activates a part of your brain called the hypothalamus. The hypothalamus is the heart of your endocrine or hormonal system which responds to your thought life. This dynamic pumping gland releases the chemicals related to the emotions attached to the thought.

> According to the American Institute of Stress,
> between 75 to 90% of visits to primary-care
> physicians result from stress-related disorders.

For example, if you feel a sudden jolt of fear, your hypothalamus secretes a hormone called CRH which doctors have dubbed the "negative emotion hormone." Autopsies on suicide cases show 10 times more CRH than is present in the brains of people who die from natural causes.

CRH travels to the pituitary gland (also in the brain) and stimulates the release of another stress hormone called ACTH. ACTH then races down to the adrenal glands on top of the kidneys and stimulates them to release the biochemicals cortisol and adrenaline. That is not good news.

When cortisol and adrenalin are allowed to race unchecked through the body, they begin to have adverse effects on the cardiovascular system causing high blood pressure, heart palpitations and even aneurysms or strokes. They also attack the immune system, making it less able to do what it is naturally designed to do: protect you from infection and disease. The hormones are not yet done on their destructive path. Next, the cortisol bathes the brain's nerve cells causing memories to literally shrink, affecting the ability to remember and think creatively. This destructive path continues until the body begins to suffer total system breakdown, leading to an emotional black hole, creeping illness and even premature death.

Thus, the hypothalamus can claim to be a true responder to your emotional state. It is the reason that a toxic thought life can affect your emotional and physical state. The hormones it releases can destabilize your brain and create a frenzy of broken feedback loops, disrupting the natural flow and balance of chemicals in your brain.

Researchers internationally have conceded for years that the role of fear, anger, depression, anxiety and a variety of other emotions play a role in causing mental and physical health problems. The medical field's solution to this problem has been to develop pharmaceutical drugs aimed at trying to change the brain's chemistry to make us feel good.

We don't need any more of these "happy pills." What we need are coping strategies to help us avoid the problems before they come up and detox our minds and bodies of the toxic thoughts that are already causing damage.

> What we need now is not yet another "happy pill" to try to change the brain's chemistry and make us feel good. We need coping strategies.

The good news is that these coping strategies are readily available and quickly accessible. You don't have to travel far to find them, and they won't cost a fortune. They begin with a thought and your reactions to the thoughts that go on inside your head.

Effective coping strategies to detoxify your brain are freely available. You can take back control of your body and mind! It is possible to lead an emotionally happy and physically healthy lifestyle simply by learning to control your thought life.

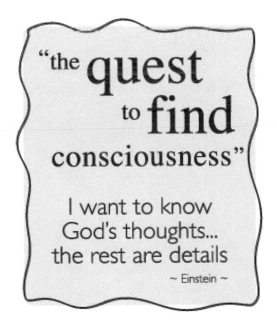

"the quest to find consciousness"

I want to know God's thoughts... the rest are details

~ Einstein ~

2CHAPTER TWO
THE GROWTH OF A THOUGHT

2

A journey of a thousand miles begins with the first step. Controlling your thought life is not about a destination, it is about a journey. The first step on that journey is to understand what a thought actually is, how it grows in your brain, stores memories and ultimately how it affects your health, whether positively or negatively.

AN OVERVIEW

Start by visualizing what a thought looks like in your brain: a tree with a trunk and many branches. The more branches there are, the more intelligent and accessible the thought will be. These thought trees are prolific. Each thought tree is made up of cells called neurons. These are your brain's functional units, electrically excitable cells that make the magic trees of the mind.

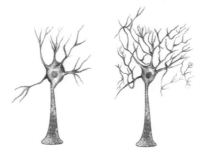

You have around 100 trillion magic trees in your brain, and each one is capable of growing up to 70,000 branches. This means you have approximately three million years' worth of storage space for information in your brain! The brain's ability is so great that it is impossible to use it up in your lifetime.

At each end of the neurons are branches called dendrites, highly complex structures involved in the process of continually receiving and integrating information coming in via the five senses. The information is translated into electrical impulses and transported across synapses (small chemical gaps) between neurons that form interconnected neural circuits.

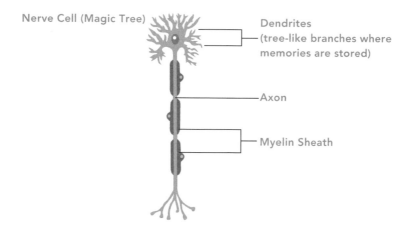

Nerve Cell (Magic Tree)

Dendrites
(tree-like branches where memories are stored)

Axon

Myelin Sheath

Neuroscientists are so impressed with the nature and function of dendrites that they devote whole conferences and books to them. Harvard Medical School neuroscientist and neurobiologist Dr. Gordon M. Shepherd has even described dendrites as "one of the great meeting places in neuroscience for multidisciplinary integration."

Spurred by advances in imaging technology, electrophysiology and molecular approaches, scientists have been able to understand more about the nature and function of dendrites in recent years. In turn, they have helped explain complex areas of cerebral functioning such as synaptic transference and neuronal "excitability."

The brain builds a double memory of the content of every thought, one on the left side of the brain and one on the right. The left brain's perspective on information processes it detail to big picture, while the right side processes it big picture to detail. This means that both sides of the brain take part in every activity, just from different perspectives. For example, when you are multiplying, the left-brain sees it as $2 \times 2 = 4$ while the right-brain sees it as $4 = 2$ groups of 2. Thus, referring to left-brain function as academic and the right side as creative makes no sense.

> The left brain's perspective on information processes it detail to big picture, while the right side processes it big picture to detail.

The two hemispheres of your brain are designed to work together in synergy, providing both perspectives of thought on everything that comes in. The more you think, the more you understand. The more focused and aware your thinking, the more this synergy will occur, and the stronger the memory you will build. This literally means that the branches of the magic trees become firmly attached.

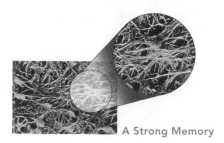

A Strong Memory

If you pay only cursory attention to the content of your thoughts, your thinking will be on a lower level with less synergy. The memory you build in your magic trees will be correspondingly weak and pruned off when you sleep by little vacuum cleaners called glial cells. This is what it means to forget.

Interestingly, while you typically have 100 trillion or more neurons in your brain, you have 50 times more glial cells. These cells generally don't get as much attention as dendrites because they don't conduct nerve impulses, but that does not mean they aren't important. We need to be aware of glial cells and understand how they work and what they do.

Glial cells are essential to brain functioning. Without them, neurons would not be able to work properly. They provide all the support, resources and back up, including the nourishment and protection your neurons need to do all that hard work in receiving, analyzing, processing and storing information. That's not all. Glial cells also operate as your brain cells' cleaners. They dispose of waste material generated by neuronal functioning. In effect, the glial cells sort out your thinking, but they can't do a good job unless you think clearly.

Toxic thoughts, emotions and the chemicals they generate can and do negatively affect the free flow of these important electrochemical processes in your brain. When things aren't flowing properly, the toxic waste builds up and diminishes the quality of stored memory. While toxic thoughts do not keep you from building memory, the memory you build is distorted and harmful.

The process of controlling your thoughts involves creating the conditions under which neuronal cells, dendrites and glial cells can do their work in perfect harmony. When they are able to do their jobs well, you build healthy memory in place of the toxic, distorted memory.

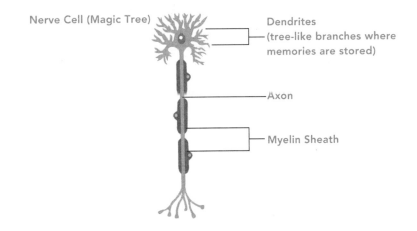

Nerve Cell (Magic Tree)

Dendrites (tree-like branches where memories are stored)

Axon

Myelin Sheath

I realize that this is a lot to take in before you take your first step toward brain detox, but there's another pit stop we need to make on the way.

FAITH AND FEAR: POLES APART

There are two important groups of emotions: positive faith-based emotions and negative fear-based emotions. Each of these groups has its own set of emotional molecules attached to it. It is vital to understand the difference between these two polar opposite groups.

Faith and fear are not just emotions, but spiritual forces with chemical and electrical representation in the body. Consequently they directly impact bodily function. Every emotion results in an attitude. An attitude is a state of mind that produces a reaction in the body and a resultant behavior.

> ## An attitude is a state of mind that produces a reaction in the body and a resultant behavior.

All the negative emotions evolve out of fear. All the positive emotions evolve out of faith. There are sets of molecules of emotion for each of these spiritual forces.

> ## Negative emotions evolve out of fear.
> ## Positive emotions evolve out of faith.

Examples of faith-based emotions are: love, joy, peace, happiness, kindness, gentleness, self-control, forgiveness and patience. These produce good attitudes.

Fear automatically puts the body into stress mode and reaction (you will learn about this in a later chapter). Examples of the fear-based emotions are hate, worry, anxiety, anger, hostility, rage, ill-will, resentment, frustration, impatience and irritation. These produce toxic attitudes which produce toxic responses in the body.

In fact, anxiety, one of the most toxic emotions that fear produces, can linger long after the threat has come and gone. Anxiety disorders are common and becoming more so. Science is now able to demonstrate the links between fear and disease and anxiety and disease, through innovative testing and imaging techniques and technology.

Another particularly powerful fear-based emotion is hate, which goes hand-in-hand with bitterness, resentment and anger and normally begins with a grievance. Emotions such as hate demand more and more space physically in the brain as well as in the thought life, causing many thorns to grow on the magic trees of the mind. Like weeds, they grow in abundance crowding everything else out.

When hate is allowed all that space, it integrates and eventually takes control of the magic trees of the mind and insidiously affects all your thoughts and emotions.

Whether your thoughts, emotions and attitudes are toxic or positive, they are represented in the body as electrochemical reactions. That is because you are made up of two systems: one chemical (the endocrine system) and the other electrical (the nervous system). Essentially this means that the currency of your body is electromagnetic energy and chemicals. A thought and the emotion attached to it (remember thoughts and emotions can never be separated) take shape in your body and mind as electrochemical responses occurring in the depths of the brain, in this case the limbic system, and in the outer fleshy part of the brain, the cortex.

THE LIMBIC CONNECTION

Suprisingly, to understand how you can start to control your thought life, it is important to understand the limbic system. Don't worry. It sounds much more complicated than it really is. The limbic system is not just a part of your endocrine system; it is the emotional center of your brain. Because of this, it is as much an abstraction as it is an anatomical unit on its own. Fascinatingly, this system encompasses a group of structures that work together like a chemical factory and can be found deep within the middle of the brain.

The principle gland of the limbic system, the hypothalamus, is often referred to as the "brain" of the endocrine system. Most people have no idea where the hypothalamus is located. But have you ever had a tension headache and automatically rubbed the back of your head and neck? You may not have realized that when you make that automatic gesture, that's where your hypothalamus is situated: in the back of your brain

How A Thought Grows And The Biochemical Reactions

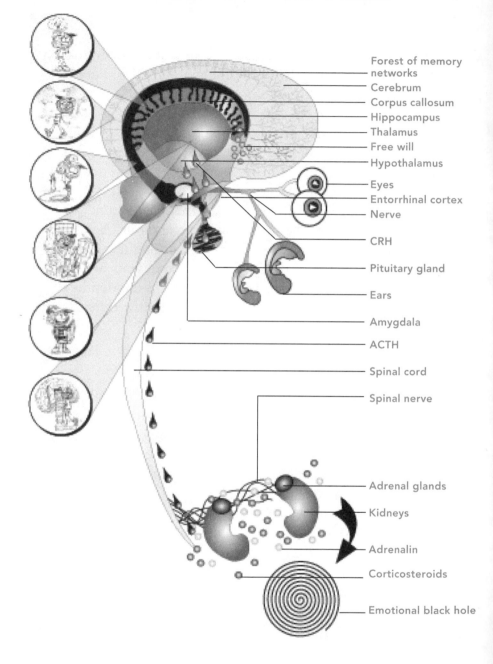

Forest of memory networks
Cerebrum
Corpus callosum
Hippocampus
Thalamus
Free will
Hypothalamus
Eyes
Entorrhinal cortex
Nerve
CRH
Pituitary gland
Ears
Amygdala
ACTH
Spinal cord
Spinal nerve
Adrenal glands
Kidneys
Adrenalin
Corticosteroids
Emotional black hole

in the third ventricle, which is at the back of your head at the
top of your neck.

Often, the hypothalamus is referred to as the "brain" of the
endocrine system because it sends out various types of chemical
messengers in response to stimulation. Stimulation comes
either from a thought or an external source through your
five senses.

What you think and feel prompts your hypothalamus to
begin a series of chemical secretions that change the way
you function. The hypothalamus also directly influences the
pituitary, another major gland within the brain. In this
way, the hypothalamus gland is actually the facilitator and
originator of emotions in response to life circumstances, such
as fear, anxiety, stress, tension, panic attacks, phobia, rage,
anger and aggression.

> The hypothalamus is a responder to your thought
> life. It can only produce chemicals in response to
> what is happening deep within the recesses
> of your soul and your spirit.

The limbic system also connects the mind and the body.
Everything that concerns thoughts, both good and bad,
travels up and down this connective pathway. The limbic lobe,
hippocampus, amygdala and thalamus also play vital roles
inexplaining what a thought is, how it grows and how it
produces emotions and physiological responses in your mind.

All these cerebral parts are interconnected and play a role in
creating a biochemical representation of a thought, processing
that thought, building memory and giving thought the
emotional and physiological part of your life. These structures
are the ones that allow thoughts of peace and serenity to put
your body at ease, or fearful thoughts to catapult you into

"fight or flight" mode, with stress hormones coursing through your veins. (See image: "How a Thought Grows and the Biochemical Reactions" on page 22).

(See image: "How a Thought Grows and the Biochemical Reactions" on page 22).

INFORMATION MOLECULES

Now that you know your brain secretes chemicals according to the emotions your thoughts generate, you will better understand what an information molecule is and the role it plays in whether or not a thought will negatively affect your health. These chemicals have an electromagnetic charge that carries a photocopy of memories developed and sorted within the mind (which is why they are called information molecules). They travel around your body affecting and influencing the various systems in an ordered sequence.

For example, when there is an excess of stress molecules flowing through the body, the first target is the circulatory system. Your heart literally feels the emotion causing the stress. Your heart, however, also has a mini-brain that operates like a "checking station" that evaluates the wisdom of thoughts, keeping rash decisions and impulsive thinking under control. It struggles when a flood of rampaging thoughts and stress chemicals overwhelms it.

These stress chemicals affect your heart by increasing blood pressure or narrowing the arteries. This negatively affects your thinking as well as the physical wellbeing of your heart. Not surprisingly, the longer this situation is allowed to continue, the worse the effects on your health.

That gives you some insight into why men in the prime of life may suddenly and inexplicably drop dead from a heart attack. Remember that the body is a system of electrochemical feedback loops that is constantly running. Any disruption of these loops shows up in physical symptoms.

This system of feedback loops called cybernetics works like this: your cells are constantly signaling other cells through the release of brain chemicals known as neuropeptides which bind with receptors. Receptors are the little locks on the outside of the cells that allow certain neuropeptides to enter the cell. Receptors are very discriminating. They only allow neuropeptides in that match their shape. This is significant for your health, because any cellular changes from an excess of stress hormones actually corrode or change the shape of the receptors which allows foreign neurochemicals or viruses to get into the cell.

Once cells receive signals from other cells, they feed back into peptide-secreting cells, telling them how much more or less of the peptide to secrete. This system works perfectly when the feedback loops are swift and unimpeded. In fact, the faster or tighter the feedback loops, the more intelligence (information) becomes available to your bodily systems. And the more healthy communication that happens within these feedback loops, the healthier the system becomes overall.

The converse is also true. Toxic thoughts disrupt the flow of feedback loops, interrupt and minimize communication and make the system less healthy. Keeping the feedback loops working well is the key to controlling those toxic thoughts, toxic emotions and toxic bodies!

> Keeping the feedback loops working well
> is the key to controlling those toxic thoughts,
> toxic emotions and toxic bodies!

THE DOORWAY, THE FACTORY, THE BREEZE AND THE LIBRARY

Whenever you read, hear, touch, feel or experience something, information from your senses converges on the lower part of the cortex, the pink fleshy part of the brain that is underneath the front of the temporal lobe (on the side of the brain). This information then passes through the doorway into the brain, an area called the entorrhinal cortex. It receives perceptual input from your five senses as a stream of electrical activity in much the same way as water flows through a hose.

The Doorway

From here the information passes into the relay station of the brain, the thalamus, which is also part of the brain's chemical factory. The thalamus relays the information to the cortex where the memories are stored (remember the magic trees of the mind) and activates these memories. This performs an alerting function to make the brain prepare for the incoming information. It is the first place where your thoughts begin to activate an attitude. I call this the "breeze through the trees."

The Factory

This alerting action happens on the periphery of your consciousness and sets up the framework for your attitude. If a negative memory is activated and alerted, then the emotional response that is carried back to your thalamus (relay station) will naturally be one of feeling negative or slightly stressed within the depths of your mind.

The "breeze through the trees"

The information then passes back through the thalamus and hypothalamus, activating the release of chemicals in response to the emotional state. Remember: the hypothalamus responds to your internal emotional state. This emotional state arises as a result of the activation just described. If there is a feeling of happiness, peace, anger, guilt, greed, jealousy, fear or insecurity, the chemicals released will correspond to that emotion.

Next, the information pours into an almond-shaped structure in your brain called the amygdala, which stores the emotional perceptions that occur each time memory is built. In other words, every time you build a memory, you activate emotions, because the endocrine system has to release the chemicals necessary for the building of memory (toxic or otherwise). Memory and emotions, like body and mind, are inseparable.

The inside of the amygdala is like a huge library that stores all the emotional perceptions you have developed while building memory from the time in the womb until today as you read this information.

The Library

An example of this in practice: if you had a math teacher who shouted at you and said you would never be able to do math, you would have stored that memory in a part of your brain called the cerebrum. Thereafter, every time you do math or anything related to the subject, you will re-experience the negative feelings of shame, hurt and fear because all "math" information first passes through the amygdala, activating the "library" of negative toxic "math" feelings. It would be as if you picked up the library book that says "I can't do math; I am scared of math . . ." This makes the "math experience" a negative one. Not surprisingly, thereafter you will struggle to learn anything new about math, because the negative feelings inside the amygdala literally block the learning process.

The emotion you feel from the amygdala is reactive and strong enough to control and even override any inherent positive elements that there may be in a thought. There are more connections going from the amygdala to the cortex than from the cortex to the amygdala. This ensures that the amygdala dominates and controls the cortex, preventing your natural reasoning from exerting its influence.

Therefore one of the coping mechanisms you can develop to detoxify your brain involves not responding immediately to emotions you may feel strongly. Rather, acknowledge what you feel, and if it becomes clear an emotion is toxic, you can begin a process of learning to let it go.

The worst thing you can do for your health is to deny, block or suppress emotions, whether they are good or bad. This makes them extremely toxic. The process of detoxifying your thoughts can be likened to "putting the library book back on the shelf." If it happens to be a life-threatening book, you may want to get rid of it altogether, building a new and healthy memory over an old, sick one.

Just as toxic chemicals are released when the amygdala reacts to a memory negatively, so are positive chemicals released when a memory is positive. If you have a wonderful memory of a picnic in a beautiful place with your loved ones, the emotional perception of love, happiness and enjoyment you experienced in that situation would be stored in the amygdala library. Each time you see a similar place, or even just a picture of it, you activate those same feelings and bathe your body in feel-good chemicals that enhance physical and mental health.

> In general, the purpose of the amygdala reaction
> is to prepare the release of chemicals
> for memory-building.

A quick note here: remember that all information in the brain is in electrochemical format. The sounds you hear, pictures you see, things you touch all change into electrical impulses, which is the way your brain likes to process information best.

THE HOSE, THE THINKER AND THE MAGIC TREES

The information now moves from the amygdala into the hippocampus, a tube-like structure that extends from the amygdala in a circle around the center of the brain much like a hose. If you lace your two index fingers between your eyebrows and make an arch with your hands by placing your thumbs above your ears, you will be tracing the outline of the hippocampus in your brain. It's a small structure, yet it very effectively holds your short term memory for 48 to 72 hours.

The hippocampus extends out from the amygdala and stretches around the structure called the corpus callosum. The function of the hippocampus is to hold the incoming information from the external world (information from your five senses) and your internal world, that is, your memory networks and corresponding emotional molecules. It does this for a short period of time until your free will either accepts or rejects the information.

The Hose

That brings us to an important question – whether or not we have free will. Interestingly, science says we do, and I'll explain why. But before I do, you need to know a little about the corpus callosum, a small C-shaped structure about the size of your thumb that connects the two sides of the brain and integrates memories and perspectives of thought.

The Thinker

The corpus callosum is an important part of your brain. This "thinker" analyzes all the information that enters your hippocampus through the five senses as well as the information activated in the magic trees of the mind. Once all the incoming information passes through the hippocampus as a stream of electrical activity, it stimulates the corpus callosum to switch into thinking mode and analyze the information in the hippocampus.

> In other words, there are genes that create what you may recognize as free will.

That brings me back to the notion of free will. Scientists believe they have identified a genetic code for free will. Professor David Suzuki, a geneticist at Columbia University says that the really important genes in your body are not the ones that tell you what to do but the ones that give you the ability to change behavior in response to the environment. In other words, there are genes that create what you may recognize as free will.

Nerve Cell (Magic Tree)

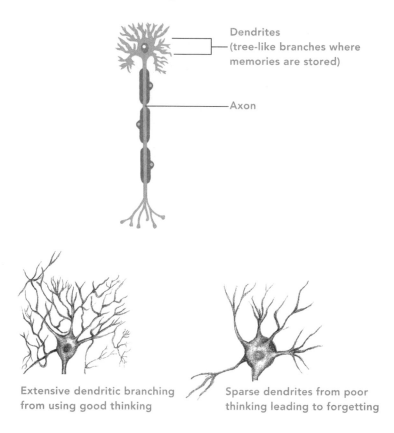

Dendrites
(tree-like branches where
memories are stored)

Axon

Extensive dendritic branching
from using good thinking

Sparse dendrites from poor
thinking leading to forgetting

Thus, your genes provide the blueprint, but they hand over
control to the brain. Because we each make choices based on
our thoughts and attitudes, we create responses different from
one another. This creates the uniqueness of every person, the
reason that you and I respond uniquely to our environment
and circumstances. The corpus callosum and frontal lobe areas
are the parts of the brain that are uniquely involved in this free
will process.

> Because we each make choices
> based on our thoughts and attitudes,
> we create responses different from one another.
> This creates the uniqueness of every person,
> the reason that you and I respond uniquely
> to our environment and circumstances.

In essence, you are dealt a genetic hand at conception that is nurtured over a lifetime. Then your individuality is added to the equation to give specific answers to how you respond to your environment. Genetics may be a predictor of intellectual development, but the brain is capable of assimilating unlimited amounts of information and then making choices based on that information. The more the brain is enriched, the more its potential will increase.

Free will is proving to be just that – directly under your control. No one can override your free will, but people, things or situations can influence and affect how you use it.

> Free will is linked to motivation and choice,
> and therefore, attitude.

Free will is linked to motivation and choice, and therefore, attitude. Once information is flowing through the hippocampus, towards the front of the brain near the free will area, the information becomes amplified. It is at this point that you make a decision about whether or not you will analyze certain information. This is an emotional decision laden with attitude.

If you have decided that a mathematics challenge is too complex and you want to avoid it, your brain will release toxic emotions and the chemicals that accompany them. In that case, whatever information is available on that topic in the hippocampus will simply disappear.

When you don't pay serious attention to information flowing through your hippocampus, at least not within the first 24 to 72 hours after you receive it, the hippocampus simply discharges the information as heat energy. There's nothing wrong with your brain doing away with thoughts if they concern information that is superfluous to your needs or toxic to your body. However, it is not helpful if they concern imminent and important information such as the time of a business meeting or Algebra final.

> It is not a good idea to let thoughts wander unchecked through your mind, as the bad ones have as much a chance of hanging around on the trees as the good ones.

Conversely, when you seriously pay attention to incoming information, you activate the corpus callosum, which in turn passes the information into the magic trees of your mind. You are then able to analyze and assess whether this information is helpful or harmful, and store it accordingly as good, healthy memory. A similar process happens when you focus your mind by meditating on specific thoughts or information.

One of the most valuable coping mechanisms you will learn in this book is how to consciously deal with your thoughts, actively accepting some and rejecting others.

> Thoughts that you don't deal with properly become suppressed and can cause emotional and physical harm.

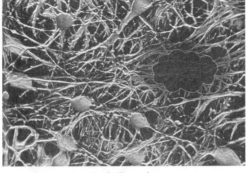

Bad Thoughts

It is also true that the mind is a battleground, with ongoing conflict between toxic thoughts and good thoughts, thoughts that serve your mental and physical health well and thoughts that deplete your body and mind of health. This battleground is located in the intricate memory networks, the amygdala, hippocampus and corpus callosum and the genetic code for free will.

A wealth of scientific evidence supports the manifold benefits of engaging in the battle, actively pouring good and correct information into your mind and body through the amygdala and hippocampus in your brain.

But what exactly is that correct information? At a basic level it is positive affirmation that replaces bad memories with supportive ones. You literally build a new network of new memories over the old.

Such positive affirmation is the beginning of changing your thought processes to detox your brain: the hippocampus (hose) receives information from the entorrhinal cortex (the brain's doorway), and all the different areas of the brain keep busy doing their own specific tasks. The amygdala (library) provides the emotional input; the thalamus and hypothalamus (factory) provide emotional and motivational input; and the memory networks provide information on existing memories.

A fascinating aspect of all this interaction, and something you really need to be aware of, is that even though you can be presented with evidence that something is true, you won't really believe it, unless you feel that it is true. It may be reasonable, logical, scientifically proven or just plain common sense, but you won't believe it unless your brain's limbic system (the seat of your emotions) allows you to feel that it is true.

> You won't believe it unless your brain's limbic system (the seat of your emotions) allows you to feel that it is true.

Your emotions are not separate, but rather enmeshed in the neural networks of reason in your mind. The limbic system provides you with feelings that tell you what is real, true and important. You have your own criteria for this "self-convincing" process which are different from anyone else's because your memory and natural learning and thinking style is different.

Your brain, mind, body and emotions are an intricately linked system operating on absolute integrity. You need to tap into that integrity when making decisions on and distinguishing between thoughts that are helpful and those that are harmful.

THE BODY'S MUSIC

Take a moment here to explore the concept of emotions enmeshed in neural networks of reason. Groundbreaking research by Dr. Candace Pert shows that emotions regulate what you experience as reality. The brain, glands, immune system, in fact your entire body is joined together by a wonderful system coordinated by the actions of discrete and specific messenger molecules in your brain, your neuropeptides.

> **Groundbreaking research by Dr. Candace Pert shows that emotions regulate what you experience as reality.**

A peptide is a biochemical that carries information through the different systems of the body, enabling the brain and the cells of the body to communicate. These biochemicals (neurotransmitters, steroids and peptides) make possible dialogue between the conscious cognitive level and the metacognitive (beyond conscious) level.

These neuropeptides bring you into a state of consciousness guided by your unique neuronal intelligence mix, what is called your "truth value." This is often referred to as the "hard question" in brain research: how do we define the unique consciousness of humans neurologically in terms of brain language?

> **These neuropeptides bring you into a state of consciousness guided by your unique neuronal intelligence mix, what is called your "truth-value."**

This interconnected psychosomatic network of emotion and reason has its own peculiar make-up. It comprises the circulatory, nervous, endocrine, immune and gastrointestinal systems and communicates every nanosecond via peptides and receptors on cells.

Your emotions are literally cellular signals that translate information into a physical reality. This happens because the billions of cells in your body are covered with receptors, little receivers on the cell membrane. As the bio-chemicals flow over the receptors they look for the ones they will fit into, much like a key fits into a lock. When they find the right match, their specific receptor, they latch on it, transfer the message into the cell and then bump off again.

Receptors On All Membranes

The message they transfer directs the life of the cell, which includes activities such as cell division, the manufacturing of proteins and so on. This process goes on in all parts of your body and brain at the same time. It means that not just your brain has memory. Your cells also have memory. Because of this cellular memory and all the communication going on all the time between the cells of your body and brain, your body literally reflects your thought life.

> Your cells also have memory.

These biochemicals, more specifically the peptides, are the physical substrates of emotion, the scaffolds that provide the molecular underpinnings of feelings (love, hate, anger, bliss, courage, contentment, sadness, joy, etc.), sensations (pleasure and pain), and thoughts and drives (hunger and thirst). Peptides are in effect the true "molecules of emotion" because they actually activate or inhibit memory-building and recall as they flow through the brain and the body.

The Factory

Peptides also create what researchers have called your body's "music," a secondary or parallel system where chemical information substances, the substrate of emotions, travel an extra-cellular fluids highway. These are the fluids outside the cells that circulate through the body to reach specific target cell receptors. As peptides trigger receptors on the cells, they initiate a cascade of cellular processes and changes.

> The peptides working alongside the building of thought into memory provide the mechanism through which health and disease are created.

Since emotions are cellular signals involved in the process of translating information into a physical reality, you need to control them because of the impact they can and do have on your body and mind.

Although you are completely unaware of these biochemical mechanisms, emotional expression is always tied to the specific flow of peptides in your body. When you chronically suppress emotions, you destabilize and disturb the intricate psychosomatic network by interfering with the peptide flow and feedback loops.

> When you chronically suppress emotions, you destabilize and disturb the intricate psychosomatic network by interfering with the peptide flow and feedback loops.

Here's how this happens: peptides do a very good job of ensuring that the immune system kills tumors (the fact is, we all have cancer cells floating through our bodies all the time). Any destabilizing of the psychosomatic network disrupts the peptide flow, which then reduces apoptosis (death of cancer cells driven by the immune system). This creates the conditions under which cancer cells can accumulate and lead to the formation of a tumor.

Another example is viruses that attach themselves to receptors. Your emotional state will affect how your body is able to respond to a virus. If the emotions you feel are toxic, peptides will flood the cell surface and change the receptor to make the cell more permeable. Any virus that happens to be sitting and waiting on the outside of the cell can easily slip in and make you sick. That is how you are able to "catch" a cold. You create the conditions under which the common cold virus, the rheovirus, is able to make you ill.

> Your emotional state will affect how your body is able to respond to a virus.

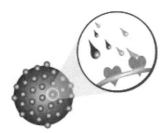
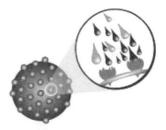

Healthy Cell Receptors   Unhealthy Cell Receptors

When you think toxic thoughts, your immune system can turn on you and harm your heart. Your immune system secretes peptides that control plaque formation so it does not threaten your health. When your emotions are toxic, you increase plaque formation in the arteries of your heart, making a heart attack more likely.

> We create the conditions for illness:
> we make ourselves sick!

Even more shocking is the effect of toxic emotion on children. Children often experience extreme stress and suppress their emotions at school. This is a common response to the controlled, institutionalized and conventional classroom situations we offer them in the name of "education." This causes the release of toxic peptides. Because the young brain is still developing and growing, it is even more susceptible to damage than the adult brain. Toxic peptides in their systems could increase children's chances of getting some form of cancer in their early 30s by 30%!

In a nutshell, the power of emotions over the whole body lies in how they integrate systems and coordinate mental processes and biology to create behavior. To ensure that behavior is constructive, positive and life-enhancing, you need to clarify the intention and emotion to create physiological integrity. If you are at cross-purposes, saying one thing but doing another, your emotions will likewise become confused. This causes toxic emotions that sabotage any likelihood of physiological and psychological integrity. This will in turn weaken the psychosomatic network leading to stress and eventually illness.

> The power of emotions over the whole body lies in how they integrate systems and coordinate mental processes and biology to create behavior.

Thankfully, science has shifted from the old mechanistic Cartesian/Newtonian view. No more do scientists view the mind and body as separate entities and thoughts as simple hardwired reflexes caused by electrical stimulation. This theory does not allow room for flexibility, change or intelligence. The shift in science now, according to Pert, is more in the direction of information and thoughts creating an "intelligence" running the body's systems.

3CHAPTER THREE
THOUGHTS GONE WRONG

3

You can't change something you don't know anything about.
If you are physically or emotionally distressed but don't
understand how your body and mind are connected, you won't
be able to do anything about it.

If your thought life is toxic, you have toxic memories physically
built into the magic trees of your mind, and the chemicals that
accompany those toxic thoughts are coursing through your
body in a myriad of feedback loops. Instead of a symphony
of harmonious thoughts and feelings, toxic thoughts create a
cacophony in your body – music that flows like toxic waste and
produces stress responses in your body.

Most of the time, you are not even aware of the toxic waste
building up in the complex systems that run your physical
body. You must learn to deal with it though, because toxic
waste left unchecked creates an emotional black hole and

moves your body slowly but surely towards ill health at best and premature death at worst.

Granted, the long-term effects may take years, but along the way, you will suffer nagging illnesses, aches and pains. Family and friends will convince you that you need to take pills such as anti-depressants, tranquilizers, sleeping tablets or pain killers, and visit doctors, physiotherapists or other professionals more often. All the time you will be deaf to all the signals your body is screaming at you, trying to get you to wake up and take notice before it is too late.

That's a gloomy prediction, but the dangers are real. Fortunately, there is light on this dark horizon. Your brain may come close to complete destruction under the burden of years of toxic waste, but it can start to recover in as little as four days! All you have to do is learn to control your thoughts.

> Your brain may come close to complete destruction under the burden of years of toxic waste, but it can start to recover in as little as four days!

THE STRESS REACTION

Stress is the body and mind's response to any pressure that disrupts the body's normal feedback loops. It is an unmanaged reaction that happens whether you like it or not. Stress is not all bad; it can be motivating, directing and empowering. However, it can also be demoralizing, demotivating and draining.

Any stress, whether it ends up being good or bad for your body, begins with a trigger that stimulates the myriad of reactions in your body. This stressor becomes a negative trigger when the stimulus threatens your emotional and physical status quo. A stressor can be external, something that you see, hear, feel, taste or touch, or it can be internal, from a thought stored deeply within the vast interlinked networks of memory. The stressor could also be both internal and external.

Toxic stressors are activated by fear, so fear is the root of all stress. Research shows that fear triggers more than 1,400 known physical and chemical responses and activates more than 30 different hormones and neurotransmitters!

> Research shows that fear triggers more than 1,400 known physical and chemical responses and activates more than 30 different hormones and neurotransmitters!

While they may originate externally, all stressors eventually become internal because everything you see, hear and feel becomes part of your thought life.

In the physical, biochemical and neurological process involved in the formation of thought (discussed in depth in Chapter 2), there is a certain point when you can control the thought and decide whether to accept or reject it. Once the thought is beyond this cut-off point, it is no longer controllable and, if negative, has the potential to become a constant internal stressor with all the negative implications for your health in body and mind.

Thus, as soon as you are exposed to a stressor, what you do next has enormous implications for your emotional and physical health and wellness. As the thought enters your brain, it passes through two highly responsive brain structures, the thalamus and amygdala, which you learned about in Chapter 2.

The thalamus makes sense of the incoming information and activates the memory networks of the mind to start the "metacognitive appraisal" of the information. This metacognitive thinking goes on beyond conscious and subconscious thinking. I like to compare this to a breeze through the magic trees of the mind.

Metacognitive appraisal is the deep non-conscious analysis of incoming information within your corpus callosum helped along by the seven intelligence areas of the brain. This assessing of incoming information is based on your existing memory networks in the magic trees of the mind. Thus your experience and emotional perceptions of all the memories stored in the amygdala kick in to assist in metacognitive appraisal of the incoming stressor.

Remember that the amygdala is much like a library and is responsible for the first emotional response to any thought.

It activates and arouses you to do something. If your "library" is filled with "books" that tell a story about not being able to cope with the incoming information, the response will be to react to the stressor based purely on an emotional level. This is why it is never wise to react to the first emotion you feel. It is a physiological response designed to alert and focus you, not to direct your actions.

Stress can be either protective and helpful or damaging and dangerous. Protective stress prompts you to swerve out of the way when a dog runs in front of your car, to defend yourself against an imminent attack, or to prepare your brain to build a helpful memory.

Dangerous stress is triggered by fear that things are out of control. "What's at stake here? Am I in trouble? Have I messed up?" This feeling of being out of control and threatened is fear based and may or may not reflect things as they actually are. To assess what is actually going on, you need to shift into metacognitive mode. You need to ask questions like "Can I handle it? How do I handle it?" At this point, you need to work out logically and analytically how you will handle a situation. This allows you to move from a reactive to a proactive state. You take control back again.

When your thoughts go wrong, your emotions rule; to overcome that, you need to learn to rule your emotions with wisdom and rational thinking.

Emotional perceptions are not reliable because they can misinterpret the truth: they mix truth and fact. Their chemical nature, when allowed to run unchecked, causes them to rule the brain. The flow of the chemicals of emotion that cause a lack of integrity in the brain immediately throws the body into a stress reaction that is potentially dangerous.

> Emotional perceptions are not reliable
> because they can misinterpret the truth:
> they miss truth and fact.

Letting emotional perceptions rule is a bit like walking a tightrope across a deep chasm without a safety net. The likelihood of catastrophe is high.

The intensity of the stress response will depend on how serious you think the consequences will be if you fail to cope adequately with the challenge, demand or problem that faces you. You might confront a demand that actually exceeds your resources and yet experience very little stress, as long as you believe it doesn't matter much whether you succeed or fail.

Remember that perceptions are emotionally based and unreliable. Emotional perceptions are designed to create alertness, to guide but not to rule. You need to take them captive, tame and control them, take the opportunity to evaluate them thoroughly before believing them and acting upon them. If not, you allow your emotional perceptions to take over and rule you. If they happen to be negative or destructive emotions, you set the scene for irrational behavior, bad decision making and harmful reactions in both body and mind.

> Remember that perceptions are emotionally
> based and unreliable. Emotional perceptions
> are designed to create alertness, to guide
> but not to rule.

Stress shows polar characteristics: eustress, becoming energized and invigorated when you cope successfully with demands, and distress, losing physical, emotional and spiritual health when you fail to meet the stressful demands.

We all shift in and out of stress more than we may realize. This shifting requires us to successfully balance emotionally perceived demands with our actual resources for coping, thereby keeping the arousal of the positive stress response within an optimal range.

As I said before, fear is the root of stress. Fear is also a very real spiritual force. When fear enters the mind as a thought, you experience physiological changes that occur all the way down to the cellular level. This allows stress to cause negative and damaging alterations in your cells.

> **Fear is the root of stress.**

Clearly, this is more serious than you thought. Don't waste another minute thinking stress and negative emotions are all just "in the mind."

Before exploring the toxic tale that fear and its constant companions of mental and physical damage are likely to tell, look with me more closely at the stages of stress that you move through. They will help you understand how and why you suffer extreme distress when you don't effectively manage your thoughts and emotions that stressors trigger.

STAGE 1: ALARM REACTION

When fear initially triggers protective stress, the alarm reaction immediately kicks in. This is the "sweaty-palm, heart-beating-fast, adrenaline-pumping, fight-or-flight" stage. At this point, believe it or not, all is still emotionally and biologically normal! You have been created and equipped to deal with protective levels of stress. The physical signs just notify you that you need to deal with that sick child, angry boss, traffic jam or any other difficult challenge life may throw at you.

> ## You have been created and equipped to deal with protective levels of stress.

Also during this initial stage, your body goes through a variety of physiological changes to prepare you to cope with imminent danger. For example, if you are about to be attacked, your pupils dilate to increase peripheral vision and you take deep breaths to increase oxygen intake so that you have more energy. At the same time your liver increases your blood sugar levels, and then your heart beat speeds up dramatically to pump the blood now engorged with oxygen and blood sugar at high speed to arms, legs and brain. Your kidneys produce a substance that narrows your vessels and arteries and your adrenal and pituitary glands make your body retain more fluid, which that then filters into the circulatory system to increase your blood volume.

All of these physical reactions put your body into a state known as acute short-term stress, necessary to keep you alert and focused in dangerous and life-threatening situations. It takes a whole lot of effort for your body to do all these things to get you into the best possible physical and mental state to cope with the threat, real or otherwise.

Once the threat (the stressor) is gone, your body begins to return to normal. At this stage, your heart slows down but still beats strongly, your blood sugar rises, the blood rushes away from the stomach, fats are released into the bloodstream and chemicals are released to make the blood clot. These less drastic physiological reactions help you to feel alert and focused to be able to respond to challenges. At this response level, you can better make a speech or take an important exam.

The combined action of increased heart rate, the narrowing of the arteries, and the increased blood volume that occurs in stage one of stress is perfectly acceptable and manageable as long as it doesn't last for too long. If your body stays under the constant barrage of negative stimulation, toxic waste begins to build up from your internal as well as external worlds. Then, instead of your body returning to normal, it shifts into the second stage of stress. After all, your heart can only beat so much faster, and your arteries and vessels can only narrow so much.

> If your body stays under the constant barrage of negative stimulation, toxic waste begins to build up from your internal as well as external worlds.

STAGE 2: NOW THE PROBLEMS BEGIN

In this stage, any increase in heart rate and blood pressure set the scene for hypertension (high blood pressure) to take hold. Muscles that would have been highly toned to run or fight in stage one, also move into the second stage where they contract too much and pinch nerves running inside the muscles, creating tension headaches and backaches. Excessive contraction of muscles decreases the blood supply further by pinching the arterioles, venuoles and alveolar capillaries that make up the mechanisms of your bloodstream and circulatory system.

One of the functions of the circulatory system is to be a trash collector, to pick up all the poorly burned fuel in the form of metabolites, which are toxic byproducts of the body's metabolic processes. When stress is prolonged, this process is compromised. Toxic metabolites such as lactic acid build-up tires out muscle tissue. Lactic acid build-up is the reason elite athletes may drop to the ground in agony after a 100m sprint. It is the reason high-achieving, highly stressed individuals experience ongoing physical tiredness that creeps into the mind and is eventually diagnosed as chronic fatigue syndrome.

This is the stage where you start to feel vague symptoms. You may not be sick enough to stay in bed, but you no longer wake up in the morning energized and motivated. You join an unwelcome band of people – the vertically ill who walk around feeling as if something (or many things) is not quite right. Like them, you may battle to put a finger on just what it is that is making you feel so chronically under par.

As time goes on, you visit your doctor more frequently. Not only do you feel vague aches and pains in places you never felt before, but your memory also slips, your thinking becomes cloudy and your creativity levels drop. These symptoms cause you to move on to specialists.

The acute short-term stress you experienced in stage one has turned into chronic long-term stress. In this stage, your mind, body and bank account start feeling as if they belong to someone else. If you don't do something drastic at this crossroads stage, you will move into the last and potentially fatal stage of stress.

Your body runs on hundreds of thousands of biochemical feedback loops. These are essential for homeostasis, the chemical and metabolic balance needed for all your bodily functions to work properly. Homeostasis allows your circulatory system to ensure a steady flow of oxygen to all your cells via the bloodstream. It ensures that your liver and kidneys filter and remove toxic waste.

Toxic thoughts and emotions disrupt homeostasis and cause structural changes down to the cellular level. The groundwork for this to happen begins when you enter stage one of stress. At this stage, your hypothalamus, which by now you know is the responder to your emotional and thought life, secretes a hormone called CRH, the "neuropeptide of negative expectations." CRH drips into the pituitary, another major gland of the endocrine system.

> Toxic thoughts and emotions disrupt homeostasis and cause structural changes down to the cellular level.

In response to CRH, the pituitary releases ACTH, the neuropeptide called the "fear hormone." Once again, chemicals like these are not all bad. They do some good in your body by keeping you alert and able to respond effectively to threats. However, when they build up, they begin to wreak havoc on your health, in body and mind.

The fear hormone first travels to the adrenal glands perched on top of each kidney. It stimulates the adrenals to release adrenaline and corticosteroids. These hormones increase glucose (sugar) in the blood to provide your muscles and nerves with energy for the fight-or-flight response mentioned earlier.

Interestingly, doctors usually wait until the morning to measure corticosteroids levels when determining stress levels in the body, because the chemicals tend to be higher at that time of day. Studies have also shown that if a husband and wife have an argument, his corticosteroids will subside within the hour, while hers will still be high for another 12 hours or so. That may account for why wives tend to simmer and seethe and take so much longer to get over an argument than their spouses do.

Studies also show that when a woman experiences extreme stress during pregnancy, the cortisol enters her bloodstream and shunts up to 60% of the oxygen and nutrients away from the fetus. This cortisol can also cause the dendrites – the branches in the magic trees that contain the memories – to shrink temporarily, causing mental blocks, those feelings of "going blank" under stress.

That's why it is so important to keep a check on your stress levels and to manage what chemicals are pumping through your system actively.

Once the stress is gone, the cortisol levels subside, the dendrites in your brain plump up again, your memory refreshes and your thinking clears.

This may explain why you "blank out" in exams, completely forgetting information you thought you knew, only to remember when you come out of the exam. Many people find test-taking situations extremely stressful. Clearly they cannot learn or perform optimally when fear hormones are pounding through the body and mind. It's not overstating the case to say that in time, letting your stress hormones rule your body and mind is like being hit by tidal waves every time you try to build a sand castle on a beach.

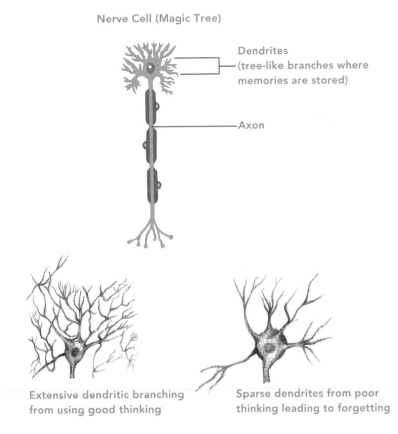

Nerve Cell (Magic Tree)

Dendrites
(tree-like branches where memories are stored)

Axon

Extensive dendritic branching from using good thinking

Sparse dendrites from poor thinking leading to forgetting

In stages 2 and 3 of stress, elevated levels of cortisol cause blood sugar levels to rise and triglycerides and cholesterol to increase in the blood stream. This may cause the body to gain weight. Cortisol also depletes the bones of vital minerals. And while dendrites may shrink in the short term, if the situation is allowed to go on for too long, they can die off altogether.

There is hope, though. The hypothalamus has a feedback loop that can quickly turn the stress system off to recover before there is any damage to the body. But when external circumstances and internal thoughts become toxic, they block the negative feedback loop that would normally switch the system off, and so the stress reaction carries on. This means that the organs can't relax and recharge because this hypothalamic-pituitary-adrenal axis (the HPA axis) becomes hyperactive.

This is also unfortunately the time when people often grab chocolate or other junk as a source of "comfort food." It may feel good at the time because chocolate is known to release endorphins, the "feel-good" chemicals. The relief is a short-lived solution that actually exacerbates the problems. Excessive levels of stress and the toxic thoughts that precede them don't only disrupt the HPA, but all the other electrochemical feedback loops as well.

Let's return to the pathway along which toxic thoughts and emotions do their damage. The stress has now shifted from an acute temporary state into chronic long-term stress, otherwise known as the resistance stage. Here, the internal and/or external toxic-waste stress levels increase. The hypothalamus is in a highly excited, hyperactive state, and releases more CRH, which stimulates the pituitary to release far too much ACTH. The ACTH dumps even more corticosteroids and adrenaline into your delicate system, causing an overload that breaks down the feedback loops that hold everything in healthy balance.

This is a catastrophe, metabolically speaking, as your system is flooded with high levels of cortisol and adrenalin that it is simply not designed to handle. And unfortunately, the HPA axis running this whole show becomes very resistant to drug therapy.

Adrenaline is also a tricky character because it produces an addictive high. Too much adrenalin pumping through your body initially gives you energy and focus that allows you to cope for a short period of time without sleep or rest. There's nothing wrong with a short burst of adrenaline; it can be actively good for you to deal with immediate demands and challenges. Long-term infusions of adrenaline, however, are not good. Quite the opposite, they are actively damaging. They cause high blood pressure, elevated levels of triglycerides, cholesterol and blood sugar, and the blood clots faster.

> There's nothing wrong with a short burst of adrenaline; it can be actively good for you to deal with immediate demands and challenges. Long-term infusions of adrenaline, however, are not good.

In the resistance stage of stress, you feel dreadful, to put it mildly. You may not even know how bad you feel, because it can creep up on you. It may start off slowly and go on for years, but once feedback loops begin to go haywire, your body can't possibly function normally. It is like your body is under attack, as the neuropeptides carry toxic messages that cause more and more structural changes on a cellular level.

These changes mean that a stressor goes on causing the damage long after the experience of the stress may have stopped or disappeared completely.

Disruptions in feedback loops are what make you feel anxious, depressed, lethargic and sore all over. They are the reason you catch every bug that comes along, why your thinking and memory become foggy, you feel tense, and your creativity level drops. To fix your problems you may resort to antidepressants, a pill to calm you down, sleeping tablets to help you get some rest, or other medication. The natural pharmacy that you have within your body that usually does all the tranquilizing and fighting of depression and infection, doesn't know which way to turn.

With your toxic waste levels higher than they have ever been, the inevitable result is a shift into stage three of stress: the exhaustion stage.

STAGE 3: EXHAUSTION

At this juncture you will be really sick, maybe even hospitalized. You will likely feel like giving up as you spiral slowly into a physical and emotional black hole.

The problem is, all your organs have been in a state of heightened alert for too long and have given up. Your adrenal cortex becomes enlarged. Your spleen, lymph nodes, thymus and immune system shrink. Your blood pressure increases. Your memory and mental functions dip drastically. You feel out of control, a failure, filled with self-doubt. Toxic waste has almost succeeded in all its dastardly deeds.

Fortunately, it's never too late to do something about what's going on inside your body and mind. As long as there is life, there is hope.

4 CHAPTER FOUR
A TOXIC PATHWAY

4

Now that you have some idea of the biochemical, hormonal pathway through which stress begins to drain your body of lifeforce, you can understand how and why thoughts and the strong emotional overtones that accompany them trigger responses in your hypothalamus and the release of specific chemicals.

When you are under extreme stress, these chemicals flood your body and create the physical effects associated with intense feelings. When those feelings are anger, fear and anxiety, the effects on your health are horrific in the long term. In the short term, there is not that much of a problem because the chemicals don't hang around in your bloodstream for very long.

Stress hormones are a very mixed kind of blessing. They are the kind of guests that can overstay their welcome if you don't deal with them. By letting them stay too long, you bury them deep inside the recesses of your mind, and the anger, fear and overwhelming anxiety eventually create volcanic build up in your body. Internalizing wounded emotions allows a seething mix of anger, hostility and resentment to develop.

For that reason, hostility, rage and anger are at the top of the list of toxic emotions that can produce serious mental and physical illness. Other related emotions, such as frustration, anxiety and a lack of self-worth, are not much lower on the list.

You need to deal with all toxic thoughts and emotions. If you don't, you jeopardize your physical and mental health, because your body and mind function together as an interconnected system.

Today, neuroscientists can track the sequence through which toxic stress carves a harmful path in your body. But it's not only modern-day scientists who have warned us of the perils from burying our emotions. The biblical reference "my people perish for lack of knowledge" (Hosea 4:6) demonstrates ancient wisdom and insight about this toxic pathway.

Quite simply, if you understand something, you control it instead of allowing it to control you. Knowledge and understanding give you the tools you need to save yourself.

Being aware of the toxic pathway in general, and the organs and various body parts it targets along the way in particular, allows you to "read the writing on the wall," so to speak. Let's track the more important ones, beginning with that very vital muscle and organ, the heart.

HEART ACHE

There is good reason that anger, hostility and anxiety affect your heart so directly by triggering hypertension and coronary artery disease: your cardiovascular system is the first target of those nasty little chemicals that toxic emotions release.

Neurologically speaking, your heart is ultra-sensitive to what you think and feel – your thoughts directly affect the state of your heart.

Toxic emotions cause heart ache. In a worst-case scenario, they "break" your heart both figuratively and literally. Figuratively speaking, your hearts breaks when toxic feelings overwhelm you and damage you emotionally. Literally, hearts break due to toxic chemicals playing a part in causing a fatal heart attack or stopping your heart from working altogether.

In the previous chapters you learned how toxic thoughts and emotions raise levels of bad fats and sugars in your bloodstream, constrict blood vessels and generally make it hard for your blood to flow. Unfortunately, the chemicals don't just restrict the arteries for a short while; they actively damage arterial walls.

Of course your body is no wimp. It doesn't just sit there and allow itself to be attacked without defending itself. It musters up all the forces at its disposal: white blood cells, cholesterol and other soldiers in the immune armory rush to the damaged site to patch things up.

Your heart also calls in excellent rearguard actions: collagen, smooth muscle cells and fibrin that help repair the damaged area. Yet it's also true that too much of a good thing can be bad, and in time, all of this activity can be as harmful as it is helpful, causing arterial walls to thicken, and the hollow tube, the lumen, to narrow. Fatty plaques (balls of blood and fat) rupture and snowball in number, eventually blocking a vessel and causing a heart attack.

As if that isn't dire enough, the adrenaline running wild in your system becomes even more desperate, yelling at coronary arteries to dilate to get more oxygen and nutrients to your heart muscle to compensate for all the extra work it has to do.

Your arteries would dilate if they could, but they are hampered by the hypertension (increased blood pressure) that makes coronary arteries thicken, and they struggle with all the plaques floating around. The coronary arteries just can't respond appropriately.

In fact, they do the opposite of what you really need them to do. They constrict instead of dilate and make your heart beat even harder and faster. You don't have to be a cardiologist to know that your heart will eventually give up the unequal struggle altogether.

The only way to deal with the toxic symptoms that plague your heart or to prevent them altogether is to start dealing with repressed unforgiveness, anger, rage, hatred or whatever other form of toxic thoughts are taking over your mind. Now, you have a medical need to forgive whomever or whatever is causing all those thoughts to run around your head. You also have to start forgiving yourself, but more on that later.

> It is dangerous to your health if you do not forgive.

Here is a list of some of the dangers of toxic emotions and the heart:

- Hypertension (high blood pressure).

- Angina – chest pain and spasms of the heart tissue – heart ache.

- Coronary artery disease – hardening of the arteries causing narrowing. This can be triggered by anger.

- Strokes or cerebrovascular insufficiency – the clogging of blood vessels so brain tissue becomes starved.

- Aneurysm – ballooning or swelling of the artery or

rupturing of blood vessels. This can also be triggered by anger.

Your heart is not just a pump; it also acts like a mini brain. Science demonstrates that your heart has its own independent nervous system, a complex system with at least 40,000 neurons, as many as are found in various subcortical centers of the brain. In effect, your "heart's brain" acts like a checking station or conscience for all the emotions generated by the flow of chemicals from thoughts.

Science is discovering that your heart's brain is a real "intelligent force" behind the intuitive thoughts and feelings you experience. The "heart's brain" produces an important biochemical substance called ANF or atrial peptide, the balance hormone that regulates many of your brain's functions and motivates behavior.

> Science is discovering that your heart's brain
> is a real "intelligent force" behind the intuitive
> thoughts and feelings you experience.

Once again, this is a case of science catching up with the wisdom of Scripture. A common theme in the pages of the Bible is the heart as a flowing spring of intelligence. Proverbs

23:7 says, "For as a man thinketh in his heart, so is he." In Luke 5:22, we read, "What reason ye in your hearts?"

Your heart is in constant communication with your brain and the rest of your body in three scientifically documented ways: neurologically (through transmissions of nerve impulses), biochemically (through hormones and neurotransmitters), and biophysically (through pressure waves). A growing body of scientific evidence also suggests that your heart communicates with the brain and body in a fourth way: energetically through electromagnetic field interactions.

Through all these biological communication systems, the heart has a significant influence on the function of your brain and all your other bodily systems. The signals the heart sends to your brain influence not just perception and emotional processing, but higher, cognitive functioning as well. New scientific evidence on the heart's neurological sensitivity points to feedback loops between the brain and the heart that check the accuracy and integrity of our thought life.

The body of scientific research on the topic of heart intelligence is becoming so compelling, it is clearly time we develop new and personal attitudes about "following" our hearts.

While the heart is extremely important and the effects toxic thoughts have on it are vital to our understanding, it is not the only system in the body that is in danger.

THE IMMUNE SYSTEM

Resentment, bitterness, lack of forgiveness and self-hatred are just some of the toxic thoughts and emotions that can trigger immune system disorders.

The immune system is the army that protects you from illness and disease . . . when it is allowed to do so. Toxic thoughts and emotions undermine your immune system and hamper its ability to do what it was naturally designed to do.

Your immune system secretes peptides, including endorphins (the "feel-good" hormones). It sends information to the brain via immunopeptides and receives information from the brain via neuropeptides. There is direct communication between thoughts and emotions in your magic trees and the way your immune system functions.

Like your heart, your immune system is also neurologically sensitive to your thought life. When your immune system faces attack, which it does when your thought life is toxic, it generates blood proteins called cytokines, which are known to produce fatigue and depression. In this way, toxic thoughts and the emotions they generate interfere with the body's natural healing process. They compound the effect of illness and disease by adding new biochemical processes that the body must struggle to overcome.

When your body faces toxic thoughts and emotions, it loses its ability to discern the true enemy. It begins to attack healthy cells and tissue and becomes less able to fight the true invaders.

A sudden burst of stress lowers immunity, which explains why we "catch a cold." However, even more ominous is the long-term effect of small amounts of day-to-day stress. This confuses your immune system, setting in motion the autoimmune response, in which your body begins to turn on itself.

The toxic waste generated by your toxic thoughts and emotions can cause the following problems in the immune system:

- Type 1 diabetes – an attack on the islet cells of the pancreas.

- Cancer – the immune system usually produces natural killer cells to get rid of the cancer cells floating through all our bodies, a process called apoptosis. Stress and depression disrupt this process allowing the cancer cells to accumulate and tumors to develop. These emotions become carcinogens (cancer-causing agents) by damaging DNA and allowing cancer cells to replicate. Stress and depression also affect the immune system's ability to destroy or repair this damaged DNA, making it harder to destroy or eliminate abnormal tumor cells and virally infected cells.

- Asthma and other respiratory ailments, such as bronchitis and pneumonia.

- Allergies – all allergies are linked to the body's immune system, including allergic rhinitis, food allergies, skin rashes, eczema and asthma. The body becomes confused and reacts to something that is harmless as if it were dangerous. Where does this confusion come from? Excessive stress. Stress makes your body overreact and see practically everything as a threat. It tries to defend itself and mounts an attack by releasing histamines from the white blood cells. These histamines cause congestion, sneezing and wheezing that are typical of allergic reactions. In some instances, the reaction can be so intense and severe, your body can go into anaphylactic shock, a potentially fatal reaction to an allergic stimulus.

- Skin problems – eczema, itching, redness, inflammation and psoriasis (scabby lesions).

- Crohn's disease – the white corpuscles attack the lining of the colon, forming ulcers.

- Autoimmune disorders – such as lupus and rheumatoid arthritis. Extreme stress disrupts the body's regulatory influence, resulting in the over-stimulation of the immune response, causing the body to literally attack itself. In the case of rheumatoid arthritis, the synovial fluid and tissue at the joints are attacked, causing severe pain and swelling.

- Inflammation – any kind of inflammation is an auto-immune response in which there is excessive histamine secretion. The inflammation is non-bacterial and involves a congregation of blood cells.

- Fybromyalgia – pins and needles in extremities.

THE CENTRAL NERVOUS SYSTEM

The central nervous system is a main target on the pathway forged by your toxic thoughts and emotions. Once your body is truly in stress mode and the cortisol is flowing, dendrites start shrinking and even falling off. The chemical balance in your brain goes haywire. Typical problems include:

- Depression

- Phobias

- Panic attacks

- Fatigue

- Lethargy

- Exhaustion

- Insomnia

- Anxiety

- Foggy thinking

- Lack of creativity

- Headaches, including migraine headaches that are vascular, from dilation of blood vessels in the brain. The same stress that causes an ordinary headache can cause the pain of a migraine.

- Poor memory

Part of why toxic thoughts affect your central nervous system is the way the emotional pain you experience turns into physical pain. Research shows that the constriction of blood vessels causes migraines and painful back spasms from reduced blood and oxygen flow to muscles. This causes feelings of numbness and pins and needles in your extremities. Over time, this constriction leads to a build up of toxic waste in the muscles, which may be variously diagnosed as fibromyalgia, fibrositis or repetitive stress injury. This has been termed tension myositis syndrome and has been linked in research to underlying emotional components.

This helps to explain why comments like: "he's a pain in the neck" (when someone irritates you), and "my heart aches" (in response to anger), are not just figurative expressions. They are literal. We actually feel them!

The important thing to be aware of here is that suppressed emotional pain doesn't just disappear. It can turn into lingering physical pain. We should never tell boys not to show their tears and make comments like "cowboys don't cry." Just like adults, when children suppress their feelings, it affects their physical wellbeing.

> Suppressed emotional pain doesn't just disappear. It can turn into lingering physical pain.

There may be times when you need to repress emotions long enough to take care of pressing needs. You may have suffered a trauma and still need to go to work, provide for a family, or attend to other urgent responsibilities. You may not have the luxury of time or expert help available to deal with toxic thoughts and feelings immediately. However, you need to make the time, because dealing with toxic thoughts is not a luxury; it's a necessity. The sooner you deal with them the better.

Repression or suppression of toxic thoughts is how we temporarily deal with the emotions that are generated. This gives your mind a chance to catch up with the loss or trauma by experiencing temporary amnesia. However, the toxic emotions that are repressed don't go away. You can bury your emotions, but you need to know that you are burying something that remains alive, and that's a horrible prospect.

> You can bury your emotions, but you need to know that you are burying something that remains alive.

Not surprisingly, your mind perceives suppressed emotions as fear. That fear remains unless you deal with it. You can consciously decide to deny or reject an emotion that is uncomfortable, but once you have done so, it goes into your non-conscious mind in a process called automatization: you first do it consciously and then train yourself to continue until it becomes an automatic reaction.

This is not the way your brain deals best with toxic emotions. Repressing them destabilizes your brain's natural chemistry and disrupts the multiplicity of feedback loops that usually expels toxic waste. In fact, unprocessed emotions impede the flow of the molecules they naturally generate (the "molecules of emotion"). When stress prevents molecules of emotion from flowing freely, the autonomic processes (digestion, breathing, immunity, blood flow) that are regulated by the flow of peptides will collapse into a few simple feedback loops. This causes the suppressed toxic emotion to become an emotional stronghold in the magic trees of the mind that alters cellular memory deep within the cells of your body. It won't allow you to function well on any level, physical, mental or spiritual.

In an earlier chapter, you learned about specific chemicals in your brain, the neuropeptides that stress releases and their effects on receptors in all the cells of your body. These substances, known as information molecules, play an important role in defining your own reality, loosely defined as your free will.

This involves what has been called the "consciousness of the observer" and is the link to quantum mechanics, the branch of theoretical physics that replaces classical mechanics and electromagnetism at atomic and subatomic levels and provides far more accurate and precise descriptions for many phenomena that classical theories simply cannot explain.

The chemicals that toxic emotions release use a coded language (strings of amino acids coded in a certain way as per the rules on the DNA nucleotides in the nucleus of the cell) to communicate via the mind-body network. They exchange information by having a two-way conversation (compared with the one-way push from behind as Newtonian/Cartesian physics suggested).

This exchange of information happens on a neurological and biochemical level that transcends time and space, and places it beyond the limits of matter and energy. That's why a cup of tea here is the same as a cup of tea in China. In effect, nothing is hidden. Your left arm almost literally sees what your right arm is doing. More specifically, your brain watches everything you do, and you are intimately involved in the processes and outcomes. Nothing goes unnoticed, and no cause happens without an effect.

Suppression is seductive as it may feel like a quick and easy way out, but don't fool yourself. All thoughts and feelings eventually come out, and along the way express themselves in different attitudes. Some of the most common are: perfectionism, a desire for control, self-doubt, cynicism, criticism, promiscuity and a tendency to overreact. These are all mindsets, emotional strongholds that influence behaviors, and unless dealt with, can take over thought life. In so doing, they will rob you of the joy and peace of mind that is your birthright.

Emotions by their very nature are meant to be felt and expressed. They are a moving, dynamic, pulsing mass of electromagnetic and chemical reactions. They do not disappear or die. Somewhere, sometime they will erupt unless given an outlet. You must deal with them, because the more you may try to suppress them, the harder they will try to be heard.

You need to remind yourself that there is a biomolecular reaction to every emotion you feel. These molecules of emotion move through the body, and if they are toxic, they will alter cellular memory, enter the cell and cause illness.

THE DIGESTIVE SYSTEM

Your digestive system is as important as any other bodily systems and unfortunately just as susceptible to attack along the toxic pathway. Its normal function is to digest what you put into your mouth. Under normal conditions, it works hard to help you get as many nutrients as possible from everything you eat and drink, to fire up all your bodily processes and keep your organs in excellent health.

There is a lot of research available on how food affects mood. Scientists at the Massachusetts Institute of Technology were among the first to document it, but many others, including researchers at Harvard Medical School, have followed suit. One example is carbohydrates such as pasta, breads, cakes and cookies. These are called comfort foods because they boost a powerful brain chemical, serotonin, involved in good moods. The comfort doesn't last long, though. Within 20 minutes of eating processed carbohydrates, all benefits dissipate.

There is evidence showing that your thoughts and emotions can render even the best of comfort foods toxic to your body, thanks to the undeniable link between your body and your mind. Dieticians and nutritionists tell you (or should tell you) never to eat when you are angry. It's almost as if the anger seeps into the food you eat as your body tries to digest it.

You are aware by now of all the stress chemicals your toxic thoughts and emotions release. When they are allowed to run riot in your digestive system, they create a poisonous cocktail that damages health, in body and mind.

Digestive disorders that can flow from the effects of toxic thoughts and emotions include:

- Constipation

- Diarrhea

- Nausea and vomiting (from excessive gastric activity)

- Cramping

- Ulcers

- Leaky gut syndrome – when nutrients leak out of stomach and colon walls instead of absorbing into the cells

- Irritable bowel syndrome – also called a "spastic colon," happens when the intestines either squeeze too hard or not hard enough. This means the food moves too slowly or too quickly through the intestines, reducing the possibility of optimum absorption of nutrients.

I wish I could say that I have told you about all of the damage that toxic thoughts and emotions can have on your health. The reality is that the list goes on . . . and on and on. It includes:

- Fertility problems

- Stunted growth in children

- Muscular tension in the neck, throat and back

- The common cold

- Brittle bones

But, that's all the bad news.

Now, there is good news, and lots of it. Science clearly links your thoughts and emotions to your physical and mental well-being. The more you manage your thought life and emotions, the more you learn to listen to and follow your thoughts and direct and deal constructively with them, the more educated, balanced, coherent and life-giving your emotions will become. It goes without saying that making your thought life life-giving as opposed to life-threatening means you will be far less likely to suffer sickness and disease.

5 CHAPTER FIVE
TOXIC THOUGHTS AND CHILDREN

5

Children today are subjected to more stress than their parents were, and much more than their grandparents were. It's not an overstatement to say putting too much stress on children is a form of child abuse. Their brains and bodies are still developing and are thus more vulnerable to stress, especially since it damages them all the way down to the cellular level.

> It's not an overstatement to say
> putting too much stress on children
> is a form of child abuse.

Excessive levels of stress and the toxic thoughts and emotions it causes in children result in a greater susceptibility to illness and disease in body, mind and spirit. What parent would ever want that to happen to their child!

As a parent you need to know that negative, fearful thoughts actually change your children's brain chemistry.

When toxic thoughts enter their minds, they create the same stress response as in adults: the brain circuitry changes and rewires in negative directions. When that is allowed to happen in a young developing brain (the brain develops for 18 years and then matures for a lifetime), all the negative impacts on health in body, mind and spirit carry over into adulthood.

Being a parent has to be one of the most difficult, stressful jobs in the world. How much more so, when you realize how much damage you may be doing unwittingly by increasing your child's stress levels.

One source of stress in children is "hot-housing," attempting to force early rapid brain growth. Scientists at Harvard Medical School are among those who have shown that parents who embark on this activity are often unpleasantly surprised by the outcome. While parents may bask in the glow of a precocious preschooler pushed to read Latin and Greek, they don't feel nearly as good when the pressure from childhood turns into emotional meltdown in adulthood.

> While parents may bask in the glow of a precocious preschooler pushed to read Latin and Greek, they don't feel nearly as good when the pressure from childhood turns into emotional meltdown in adulthood.

Research shows that children pushed too soon to excel at school, on the stage (Hollywood parent syndrome), or on the sports field, show fatigue, reduced appetite, lowered effectiveness in tests and psychosomatic illnesses. They also show a decreased interest in learning, declining ability to judge their own progress, an increase in worry, performance anxiety, and creativity blocks.

Science has also shown that early childhood stressors so significantly change neural circuitry and brain chemistry that they set up the child to be an emotionally and physically sick adult. Children exposed to excessive levels of stress before age 12, are shown to have a 30% higher chance of developing cancer in adulthood.

> Children exposed to excessive levels of stress before age 12, are shown to have a 30% higher chance of developing cancer in adulthood.

Over time, all the pushing may lead to a negative, fearful attitude toward school, the stage or the sports field. All the toxic thoughts and emotions generated by the pushing are the reason many child prodigies end up ditching the activity they were pushed into, or in worst case scenarios, ditching life itself by committing suicide.

Just as in adults, children who have high stress and depression levels have stress and emergency hormones flowing in their blood stream, crippling their immune systems, shutting down processes that repair tissue, blocking sleep and even breaking down bone.

Today's average primary school child has a longer working day than CEOs of major corporations. Now that's a sobering thought! CEOs have some measure of protection already in place from all the stress that comes with life at the top of the corporate ladder (not to mention their assistants!). Their neural structures and circuitry are already established and in place, whereas the school child's vulnerable brain is still developing and extremely susceptible to the chemical environment within which the brain is bathed.

When it comes to actually dealing with stressors, research shows that young children use their amygdala, a region that guides instinct and gut reaction, while adults rely more on their frontal cortex, which guides deep analytical thinking and introspection.

The young brain tends to jump from sensation directly to reactive emotion. This is how the damage happens. Unfortunately it is also true that the younger the brain, the more potential damage can occur.

Damage shows up in symptoms ranging from mild behavioral problems, including attention deficit and hyperactivity disorders, to complete mental blocking for self-preservation.

These reactions can go on for years and will impact education as well as the child's emotional and social life throughout adulthood.

Parents are not the only ones who wittingly or unwittingly put too much pressure on children. Teachers do it as well. They create inflexible, inappropriate learning environments, one-size-fits-all approaches to teaching that are typical of conventional educational environments and do not accommodate the needs of individual children.

> Parents are not the only ones
> who wittingly or unwittingly put too much pressure
> on children. Teachers do it as well.

Coupled with stress and hot-housing, orthodox teaching systems are just some of the reasons we are seeing more "educational casualties" – children who emerge from 12 or more years of conventional school with shattered self-esteem and few developed skills to make their way in the world. Up to 70% of these children are stressed, depressed and even suicidal. Thankfully, these children respond positively, and almost immediately, to destressing their environment.

As you learned in the last chapter, stress is fear-based. When children are faced with people and situations that are threatening and make them feel as though they have lost control, they experience fear with all the associated neuropeptide and neural reshuffling.

Fear changes children's personalities, which explains why the child you thought you knew can become a stranger in your own home. Fear is the reason children fail to achieve at school, in relationships, in life itself.

Children often appear to be fine on the outside as they cope with academic and other demands. You may even think you are "toughening them up" and preparing them for the harsh realities of life by putting pressure on them. However, nothing could be further from the truth.

Children are experts at suppressing emotions and covering up things they can't explain. It's only a matter of time before those suppressed feelings find an outlet and the child either explodes or implodes. When stress prevents the molecules of emotion from flowing freely, all the largely autonomic processes that are regulated by peptide flow, such as breathing, blood flow, immunity, digestion and elimination, collapse into a few simple feedback loops and upset the normal healing response. The results of such disruption could be deadly.

> Children are experts at suppressing emotions and covering up things they can't explain. It's only a matter of time before those suppressed feelings find an outlet and the child either explodes or implodes.

How often has your child had an upset stomach or diarrhea before going to school in the morning? The digestive system is neurologically sensitive, and the neurons in the stomach and colon flare up in response to fear, anxiety and stress.

Just as in adults, the cardiovascular system in a child's body is attacked by excessive levels of stress as well. Early stress reactions predispose and increase the chances of cardiovascular disease in early adulthood.

Quite simply, the pattern of your physical and emotional health is laid down in childhood.

THE EFFECTS OF STRESS ON THE DEVELOPING BRAIN

Science once saw the child's brain as static and unchangeable. In the 1990s, researchers made remarkable gains in understanding how a child's brain develops, grows and produces uniquely human capacities. Neuroscientists today see it as a highly dynamic organ that feeds on stimulation and experience and responds with growing branches in the trees of the mind.

This research has prompted innovative methods of stimulating the young mind. The advanced findings of this research point to the dangers of both an understimulated and an overstimulated brain. Both are sources of stress.

More than 150 years ago, insightful scholars of the human brain guessed that exercising the organ of thought could cause it to change and grow. In the 1960s, scientists at the University of California at Berkeley proved this theory on rats, overturning the idea that a brain had little capacity for change and growth once developed in a child or adult.

The message coming out of the research is loud and clear: the brain, with its complex architecture and limitless potential, is a highly plastic, constantly changing entity that is powerfully shaped and changed by our experiences in childhood and adulthood. Leading international brain researcher Dr. Marion Diamond says our collective actions, sensations and memories are powerful shapers of both function and anatomy.

Research has proven: the brain can and does change, both for the better and the worse.

> **The brain can and does change,**
> **both for the better and the worse.**

Here are some brain facts parents and others dealing with children need to be aware of:

- Brain tissue is the most complicated matter in the universe and can change for better or worse at any age.

- The brain takes 18 years to grow and develop and a lifetime to mature.

- Positive experiences induce brain cells to expand; negative experiences cause brain cells to shrivel and die.

- Childhood experiences change the brain and stress literally causes brain damage.

- Childhood is a special time where learning is fun and mostly effortless, but a normal healthy brain can acquire skills at any age. Any suggestion that a potential linguist is washed up at age eight or a budding musician is a has-been at 12 is absolute nonsense.

- The brain does not snap shut or fill up. Its potential is unlimited.

- We are only on the threshold of understanding this most complex living matter.

If you have any doubt of the deleterious effects of too much stress on the young brain, just look at what has become of youth in our modern, fast-paced societies: high rates of teen pregnancies, suicide (the fourth highest cause of death in 8-14 year-olds and third highest cause of death in 14-18 year-olds), school delinquency, increased drop out rates, drug abuse, crime in schools, failed teaching methods, burgeoning prison cells, and extensive child poverty.

Why is this happening when we have such amazing brains and so much potential? In part, it's because we don't understand and use our brains optimally. Society constantly gives us opportunities for toxic thoughts which take root in our minds and spread their poison through our bodies.

> **Childhood is a particularly crucial time for the brain because neural sculpting is at its lifetime high. Many of our abilities, tendencies, talents and reactions are hardwired in childhood and set a mental stage for adulthood.**

Our brains are also amazingly modular, that is, the different regions act in concert to allow us to hear and think. However, the brain matures at varying speeds, times and degrees and not just in childhood. The entire time from conception to adulthood is optimal for neural development because of the exuberant connectivity and neural pruning that takes place in these years.

Babies' brain growth is measured by the circumference of their heads. They go through 10 growth spurts between the ages of birth to 18-20 years until the brain is fully grown. However, growth is not to be confused with maturity. The first trimester of pregnancy, between two and eight weeks, is when the brain forms, but it takes the brain a lifetime to mature and develop intelligence and wisdom. While the first year of life is a critical period for brain growth and neural proliferation, the next 19 years are also critical as the brain develops and establishes either healthy or toxic memories.

The growth spurts and critical developmental periods are marked by myelin accumulation (the fatty sheath that covers and protects the nerve cell or neuron), dendritic growth and branching, synaptic formation and pruning of weak or unused connections. Information travels in electrical impulses across these gaps with the help of neurotransmitters.

The slow build up of fatty sheaths around the nerve cells continues in preschoolers, especially in the cerebral cortex where myelination goes on until age 10 and beyond. As myelin surrounds each nerve, impulses can move more quickly and effectively along the biological transmission wire.

The neurons are also supported by glial cells which clean, support and fix the main nerve cells. These peptide factories perform an ongoing role in sculpting and refining connections in the memory trees. Glial cells literally help us and children "make up our minds." Any form of stress disrupting the functioning of the myelin sheath and the glial cells has an adverse impact on brain development and performance in childhood.

> Glial cells literally help us "make up our minds."

Excessive stress at these stages disrupts the feedback loops you learned about earlier. Just as in adults, this negatively impacts memory formation, processing of information and so on. In young children this also adversely affects the basic skills they are acquiring at that point in their lives, such as reading, writing, math and speech.

Unfortunately too, stress is not just a problem for children after birth. When a woman experiences chronic stress during pregnancy, increased stress hormones in her blood stream pass on to the fetus. The cortisol in the mother's blood stream shunts blood away from the uterus and effectively reduces the blood and oxygen supply to the fetus. In extreme cases the reduction can be as much as 60%.

Stress hormones are also shown to cross the placenta which raises the fetal heartbeat. Studies demonstrate that the higher the mother's anxiety levels, the more likely she is to have nausea, a miscarriage or a prolonged, painful labor, and the more likely her baby will be colicky, irritable, restless and prone to illness.

Research has shown that if children don't get enough loving touch and eye contact during the first three years of life when their brains are organizing for independence, their emotional development will be stunted. This restricts a child's emotional horizon, making him or her lack empathy and more prone to anxiety and impulsive, aggressive behavior. If the trauma comes between the ages of two and five, it is more likely to affect brain regions that regulate mood and thinking. Girls are more likely to react by dissociation (daydreaming, fantasizing), while boys are more likely to become aggressive.

> Research has shown that if children don't get enough loving touch and eye contact during the first three years of life when their brains are organizing for independence, their emotional development will be stunted.

As parents, it is vital to keep a check on stress levels in your children. In the first 30 months of life, the brain triples in size. Between 30 months and 10 years it grows another 15%. Between 10 and 18 years, it grows the last 10%. In the first year to three years, the brain is busily organizing and creating the conditions for functioning as an independent person. As the amygdala and frontal lobe are developing, children who experience stress will have problems with trust, self-esteem and behavior.

This doesn't mean discipline is not necessary. On the contrary, a lack of discipline will be as stressful and as harmful for children as an excess of it. Children thrive on structure, routine, guidance and thoughtful discipline. For that reason, following biblical guidelines on discipline with a firm, loving hand is recommended.

The first year of life is critical in emotional development. It isn't possible to eliminate stress on children, however, love can help to reduce the effects of stress. Love is proven to be one of the most effective tools in de-stressing children.

> Love is proven to be one of the most effective tools in de-stressing children.

The absence of touch and eye contact referred to earlier decreases the brain's growth. So, consistent affection and attention are vital. Also, scientists will tell you that controlling parents cause damaged cognitive functions in their children, in the part of the brain that allows for independent decision-making.

Besides attention and care, the brain also needs proper nutrients and health to function optimally. A regular source of glucose (blood sugar) and a good blood flow help it to perform well. The blood flow is regulated by the emotional peptides which, as you learned earlier, signal the blood vessels to either contract or dilate. When children become "white as a sheet" in fearful situations, it is because their vessels are contracted. In other circumstances, the peptides tell vessels to dilate so that they become "beet red."

It is also important to note that when stress causes denial, trauma or fear, it leads to emotional blocks that in turn interfere with the blood flow to the brain. This deprives both the brain and the body of oxygen, glucose and amino acids (proteins that are the building blocks of the brain and body). Not surprisingly, this negatively impacts brain performance. The child will feel less alert and less focused. When this kind of stress goes on too long, emotional functioning as an adult will be affected.

STRESS IN THE ADOLESCENT

Stress is not only a health factor for young children. Research has shown that adolescence is the most stressful period in the entire human lifecycle. The media is particularly culpable here as it disseminates reports and visual images that encourage self-centeredness, impulsivity, materialism and isolation.

At this stage of life the adolescent is experiencing rapid growth and sexual maturation. Typically, the 11-14 year-old is very self-conscious while the 15-16 year-old is developing a unique self-image and independence of thought, making decisions and solidifying his or her morals.

Exciting new medical research suggests that teenagers are not able to always make wise judgments because they mostly use their amygdala, the region that holds emotional perceptions and that guides gut reaction. They are not yet fully using their frontal lobes, which guides more introspective, mature thinking. One way of helping children through this time is for parents to build a bond of trust in them from a young age. This makes difficult conversations about privacy issues easier to manage later on.

From 16 to 18 years, young people tend to become idealistic, deeply involved in issues as their independence increases. If their environment is impoverished, not materially, but in terms of love and stimulation, it will be stressful. This stunts the growth and branching of dendrites (the branches of the magic trees of the mind).

> If their environment is impoverished, not materially, but in terms of love and stimulation, it will be stressful. This stunts the growth and branching of dendrites.

As mentioned earlier, it's not just parents who are well-placed to reduce stress on children and adolescents. Children and adolescents spend many hours of their lives with teachers and others. The responsibility for destressing children's lives should be shared by all those who spend time with them.

We don't make children of any age stronger by adding more subjects, extra lessons, sport and cultural activities to their already packed schedules. Overload does not stretch the developing brain in a healthy way but instead risks damaging it forever. Parents and teachers alike need to beware of the modern school rat race where children barely have time to "come up for air."

One way of destressing children's lives is by letting them have more time to play. That doesn't mean more time on video games, computers and watching TV. In fact, these activities are shown to cause intellectual entropy. Find activities that your children turn to spontaneously and in which they show genuine and sustainable interest. It isn't always easy to find a balance among guiding children lovingly, overdoing it, or doing too little of it.

And never forget that love is the greatest destressor of all. Investing the time in building a loving relationship with your children is a far wiser investment than the time and money spent on extra-curricular activities. Overall, this is a case where it is the quality of time spent with your children, not quantity, that counts.

6 CHAPTER SIX
DETOX YOUR BRAIN!

6

Now you are ready to take the first steps on this remarkable journey we have embarked on together. I am going to give you 13 simple techniques to revolutionize your life by changing your thinking.

This is not the last part of the journey, because mastering your thought life is a lifelong process. It has no end, but it does start right here. The beginning lies in consciously deciding to change the way you think. Once you make that change, the results will last forever.

Unfortunately, drug therapy remains the main direction of scientific medical research for all mental and physical ailments that plague us these days. I say unfortunately because drug therapy, although sometimes necessary, is really only a means to an end and not a particularly good one at that. Pharmaceutical drugs, by their very nature, have side effects, and they don't always work well in everyone who takes them. Often they end up doing more harm than good.

> Pharmaceutical drugs, by their very nature, have side effects, and they don't always work well in everyone who takes them. Often they end up doing more harm than good.

The good news is that this type of neurological research is also showing the potential for non-drug interventions. It points directly to the 13-step detox program I have devised to get rid of those toxic thoughts and emotions once and for all.

DETOX STEP 1:
CONSCIOUSLY CONTROL YOUR THOUGHTS

Ask yourself the following questions:

- How many "could-have," "would-have" or "should-have" statements have you uttered today?

- How many "if onlys" were part of your inner vocabulary today?

- How many times have you replayed a conversation or situation in your head that pained you?

- How many scenarios have you created of the unpredictable future?

- How much time do you spend speculating?

- Is your mind passive?

- Are you honest with yourself?

- Do you go through the motions of the day, not really committed to a goal, saying one thing but meaning another?

- Is your thinking distorted? Are you forming a personal identity around a problem or disease? Do you speak about "my arthritis," "my multiple sclerosis" or "my heart problem"?

- Do you ever make comments like "nothing ever goes right for me," "everything I touch fails," or "I always mess up"?

If you answered yes even to one of these, your thought life needs detoxing right now.

Consciously controlling your thoughts is not just the first step in this process; it is the main step. Medical research increasingly points to the fact that this is one of the best ways, if not the best way, of detoxing your brain because it allows you to get rid of those toxic thoughts and emotions. In fact, forward-thinking doctors won't administer drug therapy anymore without some form of cognitive behavior therapy which aims at changing behavior by changing thinking.

> Consciously controlling your thoughts is not just the first step in this process; it is the main step.

Dr. John Sarno, a professor of clinical rehabilitation medicine at New York University School of Medicine, has authored many excellent books including a groundbreaking one that proposes the theory that most back pain stems from psychological problems rather than physiological. Such theories lie at the heart of the body-mind connection. In this case, Sarno hones in on how thoughts can harm the body by causing debilitating back pain.

In his book, *The Divided Mind: The Epidemic of Mindbody Disorders,* Sarno dissects the full spectrum of "psychosomatic disorders." An illness is deemed psychosomatic when doctors can't find a physiological cause for it, sometimes dismissing it as "all in the mind." While their diagnosis is right, their reasoning is wrong. Thoughts do cause illness and should thus be studied and controlled. If they are powerful enough to make us sick, they are powerful enough to make us healthy as well.

> Thoughts do cause illness and should thus be studied and controlled. If they are powerful enough to make us sick, they are powerful enough to make us healthy as well.

That's why a change in your thinking is essential to detox the brain. Consciously controlling your thought life means not letting thoughts rampage through your mind, but learning to engage interactively with each one. Your job is to analyze a thought before you decide either to accept or reject it.

How do you go about doing that? By "looking" at your mental processes. That may sound strange since it is impossible to crack open your skull like an egg and have a look at what is going on inside your brain. It is possible, however, to learn about your mental processes and then actively get involved in changing them. In fact, it's not just possible, it's essential.

In effect, the process is similar to cognitive behavior therapy, but in this case, you don't need a therapist . . . this book is your therapist. Drawing on cutting-edge neuroscience and research into how the brain optimally functions, this detox program draws on the work of many pioneers in brain research. Dr. Albert Ellis, who has been called "the grandfather of cognitive behavioral therapies," and Dr. Aaron Beck, who is known as "father of cognitive behavioral therapy," believed that toxic emotions arise from three negative and incorrect beliefs that people commonly think:

1. *I must do well.*

2. *You must treat me well.*

3. *The world must be easy.*

These may sound like harmless thoughts, but in reality they are toxic. In real life, no one does well all the time, everyone is mistreated sometimes, and life is not always easy or fair.

Toxic thoughts come in many guises. On the surface, a thought like "I must do well" seems positive enough, but only when you look at it closely and analyze the feelings it generates, you will see how this thought does not serve you well. Demanding unrealistic performance from yourself and others puts your mind and body in stress mode and thus has a negative effect on your health.

> Demanding unrealistic performance from yourself and others puts your mind and body in stress mode and thus has a negative effect on your health.

If you base your thought life on these three assumptions, the foundation will be shaky and the edifice (your body/mind connection) you create thereafter will be highly unstable. As you think more toxic thoughts and generate more toxic emotions, that edifice will crack, cave in and eventually collapse altogether as burgeoning illness and disease take hold.

From the beginning, today, you need to ditch unrealistic thinking. Keep in mind some key principles to kick-start the process of controlling your toxic thoughts:

- Thoughts create your mood.

- When you experience a fear-based emotion, you will feel depressed and your thoughts will be characterized by negativity.

- A negative thought linked to emotional turmoil will be distorted.

There are four simple techniques involved in this first step of controlling your thought life:

1. Understand how a thought forms. Internalize information about how the mind and body work together. Since everything starts with a thought, it is vital that you have a working knowledge of what is going on in your brain and body, specifically the anatomy of a thought.

2. Use your brain's natural "strainer" that increases conscious awareness of your thoughts and feelings and leads into the process of actively analyzing incoming information and thoughts.

3. Make a conscious decision to accept the thought (if it is good for you) or reject it (if it is bad for you).

4. Deal with emotional strongholds and build strong memory.

Now let's look at each of these steps more closely:

1. Understand how a thought forms.

I strongly recommend that you refresh your memory on how a thought actually forms by looking back at Chapter 2.

2. Use your brain's natural "strainer."

Activate and continually make use of the "strainer" that is already in your brain. This network of memories (the magic trees), corpus callosum and the structures of your limbic system operate like a filter sifting out helpful, positive information from the mass that comes in. It initiates a process that starts as a "magic breeze" through the magic trees of your mind, alerting you to become aware of your thoughts and preparing your brain to build new memory.

This strainer allows you to find information that is meaningful and personalized. It is part of your brain's symphony as a part of the biological substrate of thinking.

This begs the question though: if the strainer is there all the time, why isn't it doing its job? If you are not performing the analytical (thinking) process of asking, answering and discussing required, it does not filter properly. When you consciously engage with information that is coming into your brain and think about it purposefully, you literally switch on this strainer to work at its best capacity.

The strainer allows you to select approximately 15% to 35% of what you read, hear and see while getting rid of the remaining 65% to 85% that is superfluous. You aren't doing your body and mind any favors if the thoughts you chose to keep are toxic. Also, if you sift out all the good information, but allow the useless or bad stuff to hang around, and then fail to properly deal with it, you will also being doing yourself harm.

> The strainer allows you to select
> approximately 15% to 35% of what you read,
> hear and see while getting rid of the remaining
> 65% to 85% that is superfluous.

My research consistently shows that if you don't understand incoming information, you build toxic thoughts. You need to grapple with information through a process I call "ask-answer-discuss." This will help you select the 15% to 35% of information you need to build strong memory.

3. Make a conscious decision to accept or reject the thought.

The ask-answer-discuss technique allows your corpus callosum and frontal lobes to effectively sift information. You can conduct this technique by talking to others, people you trust, experts in their fields. However, at some point you will have to do it on your own. You should ask, answer and discuss your thoughts with yourself. In the beginning, you may want to do it out loud. In fact, I advise it.

There's nothing wrong with talking to yourself out loud. In fact, talking out loud enhances your ability to think by stimulating the corpus callosum to function on a much higher level. It also provides extra auditory stimulation and is an excellent way of looking at your thoughts and the feelings they generate before deciding whether or not they deserve to be discarded as toxic or retained as life-enhancing.

Never let thoughts just wander through your mind unchecked. If they are toxic, they will eventually make you sick. Thoughts are real things with substance, and as such, they need to be controlled.

The primary means of healing toxic thoughts, emotions and bodies is by consciously controlling your thought life, and that requires taking the time to look at your thoughts. It's not particularly complicated, but it is a big first step. Until you have your thoughts and attitudes under control, no amount of knowledge, skill or medication can help you to truly detox. You will need courage and perseverance to confront and control your thoughts.

> Until you have your thoughts and attitudes under control, no amount of knowledge, skill or medication can help you to truly detox. You will need courage and perseverance to confront and control your thoughts.

4. Deal with the emotional strongholds.

Memory is an important component of detoxing the brain. Once the information enters the magic trees of the mind, it is there for good. One of the very real and ever-present dangers of toxic thoughts is that they build toxic memories. The only chance you have to prevent a toxic memory is in the straining process when the information is still in the hippocampus.

Once a thought is received, a memory is built and it becomes easier to access the more it is used. If the memory is healthy, the process benefits you. But if the memory is a bad one, it hurts you every time it is accessed. Positive, healthy, engaged and interactive thinking will literally detox your brain, because it forces integrated networking and the growth of links between stored memories.

Correct, positive thinking is also shown to "grow" your brain. The brain "grows" when new connections form. Even as you get older, you can continue to increase your intelligence without limits, as long as the input is positive and healthy.

Unfortunately, toxic thoughts also grow your brain, but not in beneficial ways. Toxic thoughts grow the same way as good thoughts, but they upset the chemical feedback loops in your brain by putting your body into a harmful state. The growth in your brain will not be intelligent or life-enhancing. Instead, it will weigh down your whole body, mind and spirit. Your brain will grow heavy, with thick memories that release their toxic load and interfere with optimal functioning.

> You can literally "grow your brain at will."

Good thoughts are like beautiful, lush and healthy green trees, while negative thoughts are like ugly, mangled, snarling thorn trees.

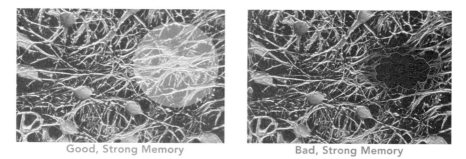

Good, Strong Memory   Bad, Strong Memory

When you set your mind to consciously take control of your thought life, you will find that it doesn't take long for the benefits to set in. Research shows that an enriched environment of thinking positive, healthy thoughts can lead to significant structural changes in the brain's cortex in only four days. While this research was done in rats, there is also research in humans to show that frequent and challenging (positive) learning experiences build intelligence in a relatively short amount of time.

My own research for my PhD demonstrates that potential can be increased 35% to 75% if people are taught how to understand their brains and to think properly. Remember, just as enrichment stimulates the magic trees within the cortex of the brain, stress drains them.

Detoxing the brain by controlling your thought life won't only make you feel better and fitter in body and mind, it will also make you smarter. Yes, one of the spin-offs of controlling your thoughts is that you will become more intelligent. Cutting-edge brain research over the past few decades, shows that intelligence is not static, but can be enhanced (or reduced) by your neurochemistry. You control your neurochemistry by your thought life, therefore you can make yourself healthier and smarter.

DETOX STEP 2:
FRAME YOUR WORLD WITH YOUR WORDS

No discussion of thoughts and their impact on your health would be complete without examining words. The words you speak are electromagnetic life forces that come from a thought inside your brain and are influenced by your five senses. They contain power and work hand-in-hand with your thought life, influencing the world around you and the circumstances of your life.

The five senses are the connection between the external world and the internal world of your mind. Information is fed into your mind constantly from these senses, shaping your thought life. The words you speak feed back into the magic trees of the mind, reinforcing the memory they came from. When you make negative statements, you release negative chemicals. These lead to negative memories that grow stronger and become negative strongholds that control your attitude and life.

I am talking about much more than just positive thinking, because framing your world with words is not just about talking positively. Your words have to be backed up with honesty and integrity – what in psychological terms is called congruence. What you do and say on the outside must reflect what you think on the inside. A lack of congruence causes stress and affects the way information is processed and memory is built.

Framing your world with your words involves replacing negative thinking and words through a right attitude shift. You do this by:

- Acknowledging that an issue exists.

- Reflecting on what is wrong with it.

- Considering how can you cope with it.

- Asking whether you can do it alone or if you need help.

Once you have done that, you can start to replace negative statements with positive ones. When you start speaking positive words out of positive thinking, you grow a beautiful new memory over the painful and often oppressive old one. Of course, you will still remember the old because it doesn't go away, but the new memory will dominate. If you don't do this process with integrity and congruence, then the positive statements will fade in time and the negative stronghold will gain supremacy again.

Remember, every time you utter a negative statement, you release negative peptides that affect the environment of the mind, and in turn put the body into the stress reaction. In effect, it is not positive thinking, but congruent thinking that creates necessary changes in the brain.

DETOX STEP 3:
EXPRESS THOSE EMOTIONS

Have you ever thrown a whole lot of clutter into a closet just before guests arrived, only to hear a loud noise as the closet door suddenly opened and everything fell out in full view of your guests? The same thing can happen in your emotional life. If you repress and hide toxic emotions, the time will surely come when those buried emotions will suddenly come pouring out. And, of course, it will happen at the most inopportune time, because buried emotions are not controlled, thoughtful emotions.

> If you repress and hide toxic emotions, the time will surely come when those buried emotions will suddenly come pouring out.

When you express emotion – which in neurochemical terms means you allow the free flow of neuropeptides – you make all bodily systems function as a healthy whole. When you repress and deny emotions, whatever they may be, you block the network of chemical pathways and stop the flow of good chemicals that run your biology and behavior.

When you do this for years, you become expert at not feeling what you feel, and you are not alone. Many people do exactly the same thing.

Signs of suppressed emotions (besides illness in your body), include:

- Irritability

- Short temper

- Over-reactivity

- Anxiety

- Frustration

- Fear

- Impulse

- A desire for control

- Perfectionism

- Self-doubt

Expressing emotions is an important step in detoxing the brain. It doesn't mean you have to "wear your heart on your sleeve" or let everything "hang out." You need to express emotions appropriately, in an environment that is safe, accepting and non-judgmental. Don't deny your feelings. Acknowledge them, face them and deal with them in a positive way as soon as you can.

DETOX STEP 4:
TAKE RESPONSIBILITY AND TAKE CONTROL

Any study of the mind needs to include, as well as go beyond, the study of the brain. The mind is like a flow of information as it moves among the cells, organs and systems of the body. Information flow is metacognitive (beyond consciousness), yet it impacts the conscious level.

Research shows that the metacognitive level is responsible for 90% of what's happening in the mind, and the cognitive level is responsible for only 10%. The non-conscious metacognitive level is where your unique metacognitive mix comes in, giving you your individuality. This is where memory building and all its electrochemical and electromagnetic reactions actually occur.

> Research shows that the metacognitive level is responsible for 90% of what's happening in the mind, and the cognitive level is responsible for only 10%.

The mind may appear immaterial, however it has a very material substrate – the body, chemicals and electromagnetic light forces. Your mind then holds the network together, 90% non-conscious, 10% conscious, linking and coordinating the body's major systems and all its organs and cells in an intelligently orchestrated symphony of life.

Your individuality implies and carries with it the taking of responsibility for your actions: you must consciously force the metacognitive and cognitive levels to interact. You can do this by consciously thinking about what is in your mind which allows you literally to access the psychosomatic (body-mind) network where the memories are stored and redirect it.

Start by bringing your awareness to past experiences and conditioning – memories and emotions stored in your magic trees, amygdala and in the peptides flowing over the receptors of your cells. Then lay the groundwork so that you can literally grow new memories over the old ones (as you learned in Detox Step 2). The bad memories may still be there, but you will have released them by removing the "thorns" on the path to detoxing the blocked peptides. This allows for healthy new growth and positive new memories. If the blockages (emotional strongholds) are longstanding, you may need extra help in the form of counseling, meditation and prayer.

The "wellness" movement was spawned by this emphasis on taking responsibility and control. Helping people to help themselves get well includes lifestyle changes such as nutrition, environment and optimization of the body-mind connection. These focus on optimal functioning of all organ systems, not just the absence of disease. The philosophy is that an ounce of prevention is worth a pound of cure.

DETOX STEP 5:
DREAM ON!

Detoxing the brain doesn't just take place when you are awake. When you are dreaming, different parts of your body/mind are exchanging information, and your glial cells are cleaning up your memory networks.

The content of your dreams reaches your awareness as stories, complete with plot and characters drawn in the language of your everyday awareness (though not always in a way that you may immediately understand). On a physiological level, your dream state allows the psychosomatic network to retune itself and get ready for the demands of your waking life. Shifts occur in your brain's feedback loops, as peptides spill out into the system and bind to receptors to cause activities necessary for homeostasis. Information about these readjustments enters consciousness in the form of a dream. Because these are the biochemicals of emotion, dreams not only have content but feelings as well. Any badly built memories are cleaned up at this stage as well.

In Chapter Two, I discussed how strong emotions that are not processed thoroughly are stored on the cellular level. At night, or whenever you are dreaming, some of this stored information is released and allowed to bubble up into consciousness as a dream. Capturing the dream in some form can be enlightening and help you to control your thoughts. Whenever you wake up, write down your dreams.

> **Capturing the dream in some form can be enlightening and help you to control your thoughts. Whenever you wake up, write down your dreams.**

Journaling your dreams is the first step in dream analysis, a complex undertaking, and worthy of a book on its own. You don't have to be a specialist to appreciate that dreams relate to your body as well as your mind. They can be early warning signs that something is wrong with your body. Dr. Candace Pert goes as far to say that the body may be discussing its condition with your mind, and you can get in on the conversation by consciously recalling the dream.

The act of simply writing down the story and feelings of the dream is shown to increase the blood and peptide flow and help the detox process. Write down everything, even the fragmented bits, and always ask yourself how you feel. As you write, you draw valuable information into the conscious mind and out of the memory networks of the mind. This is the process by which metacognition meets cognition.

People often tell me they can't remember their dreams or that they never dream. However, we all dream; it's a physiological process. The reality is that many of us suppress our dreams because of the emotions they evoke. Yet our dreams challenge us to sort out our emotional lives. Be advised: the more turbulent and disturbing your dreams, the more work you have to do on your thought life.

The crucial first step to using your dreams as part of the detox process is simply to decide to remember them. That is part of your free will, and benefits will flow. If you are looking for some practical, low-tech, inexpensive self-help as you detox, dream analysis is it.

DETOX STEP 6:
THINK FORGIVENESS

Forgiveness is a choice, an act of your free will. It enables you to release all those toxic thoughts of anger, resentment, bitterness, shame, grief, regret, guilt and hate. These emotions hold your mind in a nasty, vice-like grip. Most importantly, as long as these unhealthy toxic thoughts dominate your mind, you will not be able to grow new healthy thoughts and memories.

Dr. Don Colbert (author of *Deadly Emotions*) says forgiveness is like taking an emotional shower: it cleanses and frees the entrapped soul.

Forgiveness, in his and others' views is:

- Not making excuses for someone's behavior, *but it is* forgiving despite behavior.

- Not ignoring pain or hurt, *but it is* choosing to let go of the person who hurt you.

- Not letting someone off the hook, *but it is* leaving that person in God's hands.

- Not a weakness, *but it is* a sign of great courage.

It is often said that forgiveness leads to the ability to love. You cannot love if you have not really forgiven and released those who have wronged you. Scientific research proves that love is good for your health. Ongoing results of the "Forgiveness Study" by researchers at the University of Wisconsin found that those who develop an ability to forgive, have greater control over their emotions and are significantly less angry, upset and hurt, and consequently much healthier.

DETOX STEP 7:
LOVE — TUNE INTO YOUR HEART

Tune into the true power of love. Studies show clear changes in the patterns of activity of the autonomic nervous system, immune system, hormonal system, brain and heart when you experience emotions such as appreciation, love, care and compassion. Such physiological changes may help explain the observed connection between positive emotions, improved health and increased longevity.

Interestingly, it's not just poets who consider the heart as the source of love. Research shows that the heart considers and "thinks" about information it receives from the brain. This implies that the heart has opinions of its own. It acts as a still, small voice that checks our thoughts for accuracy, integrity and wisdom. This "mini-brain" in the heart literally functions like a conscience.

There are times when the heart submits to the brain and others when the brain submits to the heart. How often have you been told not to follow your heart? Actually, that's not always good advice. There are times when you should express your emotions. The messages from the heart affect behavior. Getting in touch with your heart and learning to live in the love that flows from it are definite ways of healing those toxic thoughts and emotions.

> Getting in touch with your heart and learning to live in the love that flows from it are definite ways of healing those toxic thoughts and emotions.

The voice from your heart is a gentle nudge, or a sense of warning. Always listen.

You may feel silly listening "to your heart" just as you may feel weird talking to yourself, but it is extremely healing to ask yourself how you are feeling. Voice to yourself what it is you are feeling deep down inside.

The best way to communicate with your heart is to quiet your thought life, control the thoughts rampaging through your mind and become as still as you can. You can do this effectively by:

- Thinking of all the blessings in your life.

- Developing an attitude of gratitude.

- Not thinking painful thoughts.

- Focusing on and spending time with people who bring you joy and happiness.

- Focusing on happy memories of good times or anticipating special happy events.

- Not allowing fear to cloud the messages from the heart.

Your heart is not just a pump. It is your body's strongest biological oscillator, which means it has the ability to pull every other system of the body into its own rhythm. When the heart is at peace and is filled with love, the entire body under the direction of the brain feels peace and love as well. The converse is also true. When your thought life is filled with toxic emotions, your heart is heavy and burdens your body and mind. In effect, your heart amplifies what is going on in the brain.

When you experience God's love and the love of people, your heart speeds up its communication with the mind and body through the blood flow. Life is in the blood as it is the body's transport system, and the heart is in charge of making sure the transport works. Health travels from the brain to the heart in electrical signals and then through to the rest of the body.

> **When you experience God's love and the love of people, your heart speeds up its communication with the mind and body through the blood flow.**

Make a commitment to walk in love, that is, the intentional choice to love others no matter what. And remember the biblical teaching that love is patient and kind, not jealous, proud, boastful or rude; it is not selfish, does not keep a track of wrongs, is quick to believe the best, wants justice and never fails (1 Corinthians 13).

That kind of commitment requires practice, practice and more practice, but the benefits are beyond belief. As the world-famous golfer Gary Player once said: "The more I practice, the luckier I get!"

DETOX STEP 8:
MONKEY-HUG THERAPY

Diana Ross once sang: "Reach out and touch somebody's hand; make this world a better place, if you can." That song is worth listening to again and again and again . . . In our politically correct world, with minefields of social taboos, we have forgotten about the power of touch.

Touch is lyrically described as "one of the most essential elements of human development," a "critical component of the health and growth of infants" and a "powerful healing force." It is the force that cured baby rhesus monkeys of signs of stress, trauma and depression, in studies by the late Wisconsin University psychologist Harry Harlow in the 1950s and 1960s.

In Harlow's research, baby monkeys were raised by a fake mother made of wire and cloth with milk bottles instead of breasts. The babies were fed but not touched, hugged or held. Before long, they all showed signs of stress and depression. The signs vanished after researchers brought in an older monkey who hugged and cuddled them. What happened to these baby monkeys? The touching broke the negative feedback loops that feelings of emotional deprivation had caused in their brains.

A vast body of research shows that touch releases endorphins and enkephalins from the area in the brain called the periaqueductal grey (PAG), and which break the negative feedback loops.

According to Dr. Candace Pert, we each have our own inner and natural pharmacy that produces all the drugs we ever need to run our body-mind in precisely the way it was designed to run. Pert is among many researchers who have shown that exogenous (originating from the outside) drugs are potentially harmful to the system, because they disrupt the natural balance of feedback loops and influence change at a cellular level.

Of course, prescription drugs have their place. They save lives. However, they are only a means to an end, and they usually have serious side effects. Good touching, on the other hand, releases the body's natural chemicals in a healing process that optimizes your feelings of well-being. Many animal and human studies show the benefits of touch, not only for depression, but for illnesses that have physical symptoms as well. Touch is one of the physical things you can do to change your mental processes.

> **Good touching releases the body's natural chemicals in a healing process that optimizes your feelings of well-being.**

You need to give and receive loving touch.

DETOX STEP 9:
PLAY AND LAUGH

Play is a wonderful form of stress-reduction. Young animals often engage in mock battles, which are an important part of their development. Like them, we can use play to act out our aggressions, fears and grief. Play therapy can help us gain mastery over sometimes overwhelming emotions. When we play, we are stretching our emotional expressive ranges.

Play brings laughter, referred to as "internal jogging" (by Norman Cousins) because it literally lets peptides flow. Many studies show why laughter deserves to be known as "the best medicine." It releases an instant flood of feel-good chemicals that boost the immune system. Almost instantaneously, it reduces levels of stress hormones. For example, a really good belly laugh can make cortisol drop by 39%, adrenalin by 70% and the "feel-good hormone," endorphin, increase by 29%. It can even make growth hormones skyrocket by 87%! Other research shows how laughter boosts your immune system by increasing levels of gamma interferon which protects against respiratory tract infections.

Humor promotes synergy, interaction between both hemispheres of your brain. Some studies even suggest that laughter helps to increase the flexibility of thought and is as effective as aerobic exercise in boosting health in body and mind. In fact, according to research, laughing 100 to 200 times a day is equal to 10 minutes of rowing or jogging!

Having fun through play is the cheapest, easiest and most effective way to control toxic thoughts and emotions and their toxic stress reaction. It rejuvenates the mind, body and the spirit and gets positive emotions flowing. Our emotions are what connect us and give us a sense of unity, a feeling that we are part of something greater.

> Having fun through play is the cheapest, easiest and most effective way to control toxic thoughts and emotions and their toxic stress reaction. It rejuvenates the mind, body and the spirit and gets positive emotions flowing.

DETOX STEP 10:
EXERCISE

The value of exercise in this context has less to do with building muscles or burning calories than with getting the heart to pump faster and more efficiently. Increased blood flow nourishes and cleanses the brain and organs. If you break into a sweat, you will also get the added benefit of mood improvement prompted by the release of endorphins.

You need to find appropriate forms of exercise that increases your heart rate. Aerobic exercise helps to sweep away the debris left by toxic thoughts and emotions. Compare that with the effects of a slothful lifestyle that is typical of the environment in which toxic thoughts flourish.

There are many different types of aerobic exercise, from running to cycling. Even better are forms of exercise such as brisk walking that allows you time to stop and smell the roses, another helpful activity to calm and focus your mind. Central to this detox step is finding a form of exercise that you enjoy. That way you are far more likely to keep it up and enjoy its detoxing benefits.

DETOX STEP 11:
DIET

Let's reframe "diet" in terms of your thought life. Eating is not as simple as it may seem. It is a highly emotional and metacognitive event. Your large and small intestines are densely lined with neuropeptides and receptors, all busily exchanging information laden with emotional content. This is why you experience what has been called a "gut feeling."

The pancreas releases at least 20 different emotionally-laden peptides that regulate the assimilation and storage of nutrients, all carrying information about being full or hungry.

Do not ignore the information these peptides provide: don't eat when you are not hungry, when you are angry or when you are facing or trying to bury any other unpleasant emotion. This will make the food you eat or drink toxic because the emotions generated by toxic thoughts interfere with the proper workings of the digestive system. You won't assimilate the nutrients you need from the food optimally. The digestive process will either speed up or slow down. Either way, it creates more toxins for your body.

By tuning into your thoughts, you can hear the messages from your peptides and what they have to say about what, when and how your body needs to eat.

Some health experts recommend controlling and reducing your carbohydrate intake, especially refined carbohydrates (mostly in the form of white sugar, bread, pasta, rice, cakes, cookies, etc). These are often called "comfort foods" because they release feel-good chemicals. The problem is, the comfort experienced because of chemicals released is short lived. Once the effects of the feel-good chemicals wear off, they tend to precipitate a downward spiral into negative feelings.

Carbohydrates, particularly in their refined versions and especially in excess, are not optimum foods for thinking. They anaesthetize the mind and dull the thinking processes by acting as a blanket that prevents you from listening to all the good news your peptides might be telling you.

You need to eat well to feed your brain properly. The brain's major food source is glucose (blood sugar) which is carried in the blood. Glucose supports the ability of neurons to store and secrete all the messenger chemicals – neuropeptides and neurotransmitters. Glucose also fuels the brain's glial cells.

> **You need to eat well to feed your brain properly.**

Your body gets glucose from the carbohydrates that you eat. That may seem like a contradiction, as I have just said carbohydrates interfere with brain function.

However, you don't need glucose in quantity; you just need a steady supply of it. An excess of carbohydrates, whether refined or in their healthier, unrefined versions (brown rice, whole wheat brown bread and pasta), causes spikes in your blood sugar levels, which is not good news for your thinking processes or the rest of your health in body and mind.

A diet overloaded with carbohydrates (especially the refined, sweetened ones), and bad fats (particularly trans fats – the ones that are industrially created as a side effect of partial hydrogenation of plant oils) will only add to your body's toxic load.

Stable blood sugar levels are proving to be the key to keeping weight stable. Proteins like meat, fish, chicken and eggs, do a very good job of stabilizing blood sugar levels. Eggs have had undeservedly bad press for too long. They are excellent brain food as is fish.

You might not think that your weight is affected by your thought life, but the truth is, it is. Obesity is implicated in the growing epidemic of Type 2 diabetes. You won't feel good about yourself until your weight is under control.

Your thoughts are likely to careen completely out of control without "good fats," the essential fatty acids (EFAs) such as the omega 3 and 6 that you get from oily fish, eggs, nuts and seeds. They are essential because your body has to have them for all its physical and mental processes.

Your body can't make EFAs, so you have to get them from your diet. Our western diets, however, are woefully deficient in these types of fats. These make much of what lands on our plates these days hardly worthy of being called food, it is so far from its natural, life-giving state.

Research is also pointing a finger at chronic EFA deficiency as one reason for an increasing worldwide prevalence of a host of diseases and health problems such as cancer, heart disease, diabetes, depression, attention deficit and hyperactivity problems in children. Think about what and why you are eating. It is an important part of controlling your thoughts.

> **Think about what and why you are eating. It is an important part of controlling your thoughts.**

Many health experts also advise drinking lots of water for optimum function of all body systems. Water has been called "God's nectar," and at the risk of stating the obvious, you cannot live without it. Within three days of not drinking water, the membranes on your brain will be irreversibly affected, and within seven days of not drinking, you will be dead.

When you feel hungry, sip some hot or cold water to determine whether you are thirsty or hungry. If you are genuinely hungry, the water will prepare your body for digestion.

And remember: toxic thoughts give you toxic emotions which give you toxic bodies. It's a combination of the correct principles of eating, combined with the correct attitude to eating, that will allow you to move toward detoxing.

DETOX STEP 12:
THE SPIRITUAL ASPECT

You are a spiritual being. No healing of toxic waste in your mind and body will be complete unless you address this spirituality. I have found that science is not antagonistic to spirituality. To me, it even confirms the power of and has developed my spiritual life.

Without a doubt, my Christianity is the guiding belief of my life. It gives me hope in a world that is often without hope, and a truth and reality to anchor in. God is my Intelligent Designer, and the level of information that is flowing is the Holy Spirit.

In a sense, it is not energy acting on matter to create behavior, but intelligence in the form of information running all the systems and creating behavior. This, for me, is the Holy Spirit. Spirituality moves away from the ultimate mechanical godless universe peopled by clocklike organisms as conceived by the Cartesian and Newtonian models. It is instead an intelligent information network run by an Intelligent Designer, conceived on a level where only faith operates. I challenge you to find your spiritual truth to deal with toxic emotions.

DETOX STEP 13:
RELAX!

Rush, rush, rush! Hurry, hurry, hurry! Busy, busy, busy! This is the song that the world chants these days. It is changing the way we conceive time. Do you often feel as if time is not just flying by, but streaking past you faster than the speed of light? Once again, you are not alone. It's a global phenomenon, and just one area of our lives that is suffering is our thought life.

The ever-increasing pace of life is called the "acceleration syndrome," and it is causing a global epidemic of hurry sickness. One of the symptoms is the dizzying speed at which we live and the amount of living we are forcing into our lives.

Many "solutions" offered, such as time management and learning to delegate and prioritize, are having the opposite effect. They are actually increasing the pace of life, creating a time squeeze in which we are encouraged to cram even more into an hour. They only aggravate the problem they are supposed to be addressing.

They make you time poor, and that poverty is extending to your thought life. Your time is precious, and it belongs only to you. Every day you make choices about how you are going to spend your time. Learning to spend it wisely is an important part of controlling your thoughts.

The next time you think you don't have time for exercise or relaxation, think again. The reality is simply that you have chosen to fill your time with activities and things other than exercise and relaxation. Focus on what is good for you. Like many of us, you manage to fill your day with an endless list of things, small or large, which are not vital to your interests. If you constantly focus on the little things, you may ignore the big things that ultimately determine your health, success and happiness.

> The next time you think you don't have time for exercise or relaxation, think again. The reality is simply that you have chosen to fill your time with activities and things other than exercise and relaxation.

Every organ and muscle in our body has a sympathetic or stress state and a parasympathetic or relaxed state. Both of these systems are part of the autonomic nervous system. Researchers at the Institute of HeartMath (an organization that researches the effects of positive emotions on physiology and quality of life and performance) have found that the toxic emotions experienced as a result of this "busy-rush syndrome" cause disruptions to the autonomic nervous system that lead to erratic heart rhythms (among a myriad of other health problems).

Take the time to do things that generate positive emotions, such as love, respect and kindness, and the result will be more coherent heart rhythms. This rhythm is a balance between the sympathetic (accelerates the heartbeat) and the parasympathetic (slows down the heartbeat) nervous systems. Therefore, relaxing is not just a luxury, it's a necessity. You need to balance the sympathetic and parasympathetic systems. Toxic thoughts throw this balance off and predispose you to sickness.

Learn to balance your work and rest before it's too late. Make a list of what you would eliminate from your life if you only had six months to live. I suggest you include what you would really like to do in those six months to make you as happy and content as possible. You will be amazed both at how much dross you will cut out of your daily schedule and what important things you have been keeping out of it!

> ## Learn to balance your work and rest before it's too late.

Twenty-five years ago, a cardiologist at Harvard University Medical School, Dr. Herbert Bensen, described a physiological reaction that he called the relaxation-response. He gave a modern name to an idea that is as old as the hills of ancient Greece and runs through many ancient traditional healing systems.

Some techniques that help with inducing the relaxation-response include:

- Deep breathing

- Progressive muscle relaxation – moving through your different muscle groups tensing and relaxing from your head to your toes

- Stretching and relaxing

- Imagining (visualizing) – for example, a relaxing scene like walking along a beach

- Meditation – focused awareness, interactive and engaged positive thinking with understanding as a result

- Prayer

- Massage (it's part of touch therapy)

- Aerobic exercise – brisk walking, cycling, swimming, jumping with reasonable intensity

- Daily quiet time all to yourself, with little or nothing to do but relax

- Sleep – the ultimate relaxer! You need between seven to nine hours of sleep a night, and more on the weekends. If you are one of the many walking around chronically sleep deprived, you need to address that. Quality and quantity of restful sleep are prerequisites for controlling toxic thoughts.

Epilogue

This is a book about a battle: the battle for your mind. It's almost an unfair battle because you can't see what's happening, yet you simply can't get away from the war. You are in the midst of it whether you like it or not!

The battle's starting line is the toxic thought, and the finishing line is the final battle cry of victory when you control and overturn the toxic thought.